365 Days of Motivation

365 Days of Motivation

ERNEST L. SLEDGE

The Baobab Press, LLC

Pontiac, Michigan
2013

365 Days of Motivation

by Ernest L. Sledge
edited by Candy R. Geeter
Cover Design by: D'Artagnan Burris

Published in the United States by:
The Baobab Press, LLC

THE BAOBAB PRESS, LLC

Pontiac, MI
www.thebaobabpress.com

ISBN: 978-0-9893757-7-1

Join the movement that replaces fear with peace and worry with encouragement. This book will transform your mindset and provide you with a lifelong membership to #TeamNoFear.

God is faithful, and he will allow you to be tested, but not beyond what you can endure. Just before you reach your actual breaking point, God will send you an encouraging word. This book is 365 days of encouragement. When fear threatens to steal your peace, allow these practical words to inspire you. May every word strengthen you and bless you, so that you may continue to resist the enemy and claim victory over any situation!

Today's Word

BATTLEFIELD UPDATE

Brothers are turning on brothers and sisters, turning on sisters to kill them naturally and spiritually. So-called Christian leaders are selling out for this paper we call money with the result being millions of misguided souls. There is a selfishness that runs rapidly throughout the land. And the spirit of the antichrist has gotten bolder with the passing of each day. But there is a P.O.R. (Pocket of Resistance), and I am from that resistances, known as **#TeamNoFear**, and here is the message that I am transmitting...

Brothers and Sisters hold fast to your faith and the Word of God and his promises. Know that the Lord of our salvation will deliver you in your time of need if you faint not. Be clear on your intentions and stand firm in your faith, knowing that the result is victory. Surrender to God entirely and be open and honest. It will do you no good to hide anything, for he knows all and sees all. Always stay fully armored and on guard, for our enemy looks for any opportunity to spill blood. May this message reach you in your time of need **#TeamNoFear**

Day 1

TODAY'S WORD! You have the choice not to feed the spirit of violence. Today is your chance to begin to starve it. STOP letting the devil use your mouth to speak. Stop being a part of negativity and start disconnecting yourself from people who love that type of environment. Words can do significant damage. At times words can do more damage than physical harm. And sometimes, it takes years to get over the hurt and begin to heal. Suppose you find yourself loving to watch TV shows/sitcoms with drama (profanity, violence, backbiting, and lying) or others, which feed a violent spirit, check yourself. You are doing nothing but planting this seed of corruption in your spirit, and it will begin to grow and manifest itself in your life. This message is not for everyone, but those of you who understand the dynamics of spiritual warfare; this message is loud and clear. Therefore, I say, do all you can to give yourself an advantage against your adversary. Disconnect yourself from useless and unproductive people or things. #TeamNoFear

Day 2

TODAY'S WORD! Learning to be comfortable no matter where God has, you will not happen overnight. It is a process and takes time, but remain patient and diligent in prayer, and all things will work in your favor. Whether you are in the desert or the valley, stay patient. Whether you are climbing a mountain or in the rain, remain patient. Through prayer, the victory will be yours. Many allow where they are to dictate the way they feel and think. By doing so, they miss out on the lesson/message that God is trying to speak to them at that time. Therefore, focus on where you are going and not where you are. Continue to have faith and move forward in what God has for you. **#TeamNoFear**

Day 3

TODAY'S WORD! Why worry about things you cannot control? Why get upset about things other people do? Today and tomorrow will take care of itself, so with that being said, you are to take care of YOURSELF and focus on what God has you to do. You were created for a purpose. God had a plan when he made you. Getting focus requires you to remove

8

distractions from people and things. So clean house today and focus. You have work to do. #TeamNoFear

Day 4

TODAY'S WORD! Don't focus on where you are but focus on where you're going. God will supply your needs, so continue to move forward. Walk-in truth and be honest with yourself and your fellow brother and sister. Don't waste your time and energy on nonsense. Continue with your work. Never let what you see or feel cause you to doubt God's Word. Stand on his word and his promises during the darkest hour, and he will bring you out. Know that God is not done with you yet! **#TeamNoFear**

Day 5

TODAY'S WORD! Know that God did not bring you out this far to take you back again. STOP LOOKING BACK! He is preparing you for a job, and through your trials and tribulations, you are made stronger. Can a professional bodybuilder get a physique like the one he or she has without sacrificing, working out, being committed, and going through some pain? So how can your faith grow if it is not being worked out, stretched, and tested? God has a plan for you. Take the time to find out what it is by praying and STOP complaining. Look for God instead of looking at your problems. Speak God's Word instead of doubt and unbelief. Listen to the Holy Spirit instead of words from the mouths of liars. Move forward in the Lord, amid whatever you may face, and you will find victory. **#TeamNoFear**

Day 6

TODAY'S WORD! I come today to remind you that our God is awesome and that he is able. No matter where you are or what you may be going through, BE ENCOURAGED! Allow God to give you a testimony of victory. There is no storm too big! There is no enemy too powerful! There is no situation too hard for God to work out. For his ways are not our ways, and neither are his thoughts our thoughts. He is able, and if you choose to stand on God's Word during your time of trouble, God will do whatever has to be done. Know that giving up is

10

NOT an option! So, continue to stand while God works his plan for your life. Today is your day of victory! **#TeamNoFear**

Day 7

TODAY'S WORD! What will your legacy be when you die? How will you be remembered? What will be said about you when you're gone? What will your work say about you? How will family and friends talk after you are gone? How will the lives of those you have touched been changed? What you do in this life will echo into eternity. So, stop wasting your time and energy on nonsense. You have work to do. **#TeamNoFear**

Day 8

TODAY'S WORD! The minute you realize that this life is temporary, the sooner you will see those things that are so precious and important. Some will chase after millions but neglect the fact that they are healthy. Many work to pile up tons of material possessions but ignore the fact that they have their sight and use of all their limbs. Cars get into accidents, homes burn down, and money gets spent or stolen. Even the body you live in dies daily and grows old until it is no longer of use. Therefore, focus on that which is eternal and everlasting, leaning not on material things that will soon perish. Be thankful for that which you have, which is unable to be taken away. Be grateful for what God has given you, which man is not able to charge you. Tap into who you are destined to be, releasing the blessing you have for yourself and the rest of the world. Be watchful and protect that which is of great value. May your ears be unplugged that you may hear. May your eyes be opened that you may see. And may your heart be receptive that you may understand greater is that which God has given and not man. **#TeamNoFear**

Day 9

TODAY'S WORD! Know that you are destined for greatness, and you are on an assignment from God to complete a task. Therefore, you have no time to waste on nonsense. Nor time to spend affiliating yourself with people who will hinder your progress. Spend your time preparing yourself by renewing your mind with the Word of God. Seeking God's knowledge will enable you to detect nonsense and people that are only sent to steal your precious time. You have a choice, so choose to prepare or choose to fail. The time will continue to tick, and the days will continue to pass. So, I say to you today, GET YOUR WORK DONE. **#TeamNoFear**

Day 10

TODAY'S WORD! How do you expect things to change when you are thinking the same and speaking the same? How do you expect to improve when you continue to repeat those wrong choices? Look in the mirror, and today tell that person enough is enough! You have held me back long enough; you have kept me from my blessing long enough. You have hindered my progress and have discouraged me in every way possible. By filling me with fear and doubt, you have talked me out of my dreams and goals. Today I tell you, I will no longer listen to you. I will stand in agreement with the word of God from here on out. So, I say to all of my Facebook friends, it's time to BREAK UP WITH YOURSELF.

Day 11

TODAY'S WORD! Be encouraged for the Lord, our God sees you and knows your heart and your intentions. He is preparing you for greater and moving you into victory. "Fear neither the words your enemy may speak nor the report they may read. For if you choose this day to stand and believe in My Word, I will move mountains," said the Lord. I will cause your enemies to scatter and be confused. I will use those who plan to set you up for failure to be the reason you will succeed. I will cause the rain to fall and water every seed you have sown. Today victory will be in your standing! I have heard your prayers, and I have seen your situation. There is nothing too hard or too difficult for me to fix or turn around. So, I say unto you STAND amid this turmoil and remain standing in the presence of your enemies and watch me bring you into victory. SAID THE LORD! #TeamNoFear

Day 12

TODAY'S WORD! There are people assigned to get on your nerves and under your skin. They plan to waste your time and resources on nonsense. They also plot and plan to get you away from your prayer and study time by having you on the phone for hours. There are things in place to keep you stagnant in one place to rot and sour. And now that you know this KNOW YOUR ENEMY AND PLAN ACCORDINGLY. #TeamNoFear

Day 13

TODAY'S WORD! Never take for granted that this is the day that the Lord has made. Instead, ask yourself, why are you here? What are you supposed to be doing? Where are you going? These are questions that you should have answers to, and the only way to get those answers is to seek the Lord daily. Did you know that you have a purpose? You have a destiny. There is a reason why you are here and why you were created. It is sad to say, but many people will never take the time to find out what's their purpose. The snares and pitfalls of this world keep them entertained with useless nonsense. They seek drama and waste large amounts of valuable time in gossip. The choice is yours. HOW WILL YOU SPEND YOUR TIME TODAY? **#TeamNoFear**

Day 14

TODAY'S WORD! Be glad and rejoice in this is the day, which the Lord has made! The breath of life is once again in you, allowing you to get up and get started on your task at hand. LISTEN! What comes out of your mouth affects your thinking, and your thinking will affect your actions. Therefore, be transformed by the renewing of your mind, putting your words in line with God's Word, and your thinking will automatically follow suit. Eventually, your actions will change in alignment with God's Word. There is no time to waste on petty nonsense that comes only to sow seeds of repeating failure. Going over the same lesson and learning nothing is a waste of time. Therefore, listen, hear, and learn. Change accordingly and then allow those changes to take you in the right direction. You are heading towards your destiny and purpose. Tame your tongue, control your mouth, and renew your thinking. Your task is at hand. **#TeamNoFear**

Day 15

TODAY'S WORD! Consider a warrior and the fact that he or she must train and sacrifice to be successful in battle. Mental and physical exercise is of utmost importance and is essential when it comes to victory. So how can one expect to win when you get out of the bed with the wrong attitude and mindset? You are already defeated and heading in the wrong direction. A warrior looks forward to battle because he or she knows they are prepared for such a time as this. There are many fighters, but few warriors in the kingdom of God. So, choose this day, which one you are, and act accordingly. Start your training! Study, Pray, and Execute the WORD OF GOD! **#TeamNoFear**

Day 16

TODAY'S WORD! If you continue to think the same, you will continue to act the same. If you continue to speak, the same things will continue to happen. How can one expect to reap apples when the seeds he or she has planted are those of oranges? It is simple. STOP making it so complicated and STOP making excuses. You choose what or whom you allow in your life and the things you are a part of, whether negative or positive, evil or good. What or who have you been listening to? What or who have you been watching? You get out what you put in, so if you put in junk, trash is coming out. Make a conscious decision today and ask yourself, how is this benefiting me? Your purpose for being here just may be in jeopardy because you choose to waste your time and energy on nonsense. **#TeamNoFear**

Day 17

TODAY'S WORD! What or who do you support? What or whom are you listening to and watching? What are you reading, and what is the message being conveyed? Do you feed the spirit or flesh more? The fruits of your life are a result of the answers to these questions. Cause and effect! You reap what you sow! You get out what you put in! God gave you the power to choose, and the choices that you make are up to you. So, watch, listen, and read whatever you may desire, but keep this in mind. You are planting seeds, and those seeds will eventually grow positive or negative and evil or good. Today's weather forecast is calling for rain! I hope you have the right seeds in the ground. **#TeamNoFear**

Day 18

TODAY'S WORD! Make plans to change into a better you; without a change, your growth has been hindered. How is that possible? For if any man or woman is in Christ, they are a NEW CREATURE, right? So how are you falling for the same old tricks? Why do the same old things continue to get under your skin? How is it possible for the enemy to continue to use your mouth to speak? Has there been any growth? LISTEN! God WILL NOT just take over and control you like a mindless zombie. You must work! You must seek it! You must pray! You must surrender! You must study! You must pursue the things of God. If you are not committed to doing this, and it sounds like too much work, I guess you will continue to be the same old you. You are repeating the same old behavior over and over. My prayer is that you will get tired of doing that and DO SOMETHING differently! **#TeamNoFear**

Day 19

TODAY'S WORD! Your life has a purpose; you have been allowed to see this day for a reason. It was not to get upset, and it was not to continue to be a victim. The circumstances and the situations you face daily come to make you stronger and wiser. You must learn from your mistakes so that you will not continue to fall into a vicious cycle of repetitiveness. You have to make a decision that you want better, and you will do better. You must say that! You must believe that! Then you will do that! Habits can be helpful, or they can be a hindrance, you must decide which habits are helpful and which are not. You can then begin to execute your plan of action; after all, NO WORK, NO REWARD! **#TeamNoFear**

Day 20

TODAY'S WORD! Listen, God, WILL NOT just step in and take over, making everything a cakewalk for you. If he did, how can your faith grow? Be not deceived; there is a HUGE difference between *knowing God* and *knowing of God*. There is an even bigger difference between *religion* and *relationship*. If your mind has been renewed, why does your mouth continue to speak the same words? How does your thinking remain the same? Consider a bodybuilder; if he or she does not expect a physical change, they will continue to eat the same and will not put in the necessary work to make the change. Your spirit man is the same way but without laziness. So, where does the laziness come from? There is NO cake walking, so STOP complaining and STOP expecting things to change if you are going to continue to speak and think the same. **#TeamNoFear**

Day 21

TODAY'S WORD! Having the right attitude can take you a long way knowing that all things that happen in your life have a purpose. Consider Job; he had the right attitude and mindset, which was all tied together with faith. How can you expect to be blessed when your view is always "Lord, why me?" Every time your faith is tested, you cry WHY ME, but your prayer should "Lord, I want to be closer to you." How can you expect to get closer to God without your faith being tested? How can you expect your seeds to grow when there is no rain? How can you expect things to change when you continue to speak words of negativity and defeat? You will never see an eagle flying with crows, so why would you continue to waste your time with garbage pickers? Adjust your mindset and fix your attitude. Check your mouth and get in line with the word so that you may get closer to God. **#TeamNoFear**

Day 22

TODAY'S WORD! Listen! You have to realize that while you woke up this morning hoping for the best, there are people whose plan is to cause destruction and as much chaos as possible working on getting closer to your dreams and goals. Some people are the opposite; they plan to cause destruction and as much chaos as possible. As soon as you realize that everyone is not your friend and everyone will not support you, the sooner you will understand who and what you are fighting against. War is not fun or easy; however, you must grow and have peace. So, STOP complaining about what other people say and do. They are saying and doing what they have planned. Are you? They have a strategy for success and victory, do you? How are you preparing? What are your time and energy spent on? Thinking smarter will lead to being smarter! Speaking victory will lead to obtaining victory! Therefore, every morning it is in your best interest to leave your home prepared. Read, Study, and Pray. **#TeamNoFear**

Day 23

TODAY'S WORD! You are destined for greatness, so do not waste your precious time on nonsense. There is a plan for your failure that is tailored made to fit you, courtesy of your adversary. This is a game of chess, not checkers. You must be prepared for battle every day, physically and spiritually. Know that everything you need for success is at your disposal; however, the flesh is weak, but the spirit is willing. The flesh is lazy and unwilling to cooperate, but the spirit is ready and willing. You must surrender and press on to obtain victory. Half the battle is focusing and knowing that you will face opposition every time you leave your home. You are at war, so be smart and have a plan. Never fight blind, and don't allow your mouth to defeat you with words of failure and hopelessness. The seeds of doubt are planted and grow into trees of fear that block the SON. #TeamNoFear

Day 24

TODAY'S WORD! Falling teaches you how to avoid falling again; it also teaches you how to get back up. You learn to crawl, walk, and eventually, you are running. Don't beat yourself up in the learning process; just put forth your most considerable effort. The Lord, our God, will never leave you nor forsake you, so in that have faith. By confessing today that you are delivered and blessed, you are! Cast down every thought that will come to hinder and hold you back. Believe not the words of your enemy; neither trust his actions for his intentions are evil. Walk with your eyes open and your mind transparent and renewed so that you may be ready. The spirit is willing, but the flesh is weak, so surrender to that which is good and favorable. And lean not to your understanding but trust the Lord in all your ways, and he will direct your path. So today, put forth your best effort in the most significant walk of your life. #TeamNoFear

Day 25

TODAY'S WORD! If you can bless someone today, why wouldn't you look to be a blessing? Search for a kind word to speak to someone today because they may be in the middle of a storm. Life and death are in the power of the tongue, and faith comes by hearing. Are your words bringing death or creating life? Are your words helping or hindering your neighbor? Setting yourself up for a blessing starts by blessing someone else. You reap what you sow. You are the light during darkness and hope amid hopelessness. So, allow God to use you to get his work done and reach those who are lost. Be receptive to receive his guidance so that you may fulfill your purpose. And do not let nonsense block your ability to hear his plan. Today is your chance to be a blessing!

Day 26

TODAY'S WORD! How will you be remembered? What words will follow your name once you die? What type of conversations will your name be attached to? What type of legacy will you leave, if any? Words whispered or spoken out loud; what message will they contain? One thing is for certain that what you do in life will echo in eternity. Therefore, put forth your greatest effort in all that you do and always make your intentions clear. Be honest with your fellow neighbor so that good things may be returned to you. Lend a helping hand whenever possible so that in your time of need, you may have a hand extended towards you. Don't hide your faults but exposed them so that you may grow and help others. Many people spend a lifetime trying to fill a cup with a hole in the bottom. By fixing the hole, so that the water doesn't leak out, you bring life to yourself and others around you. So, I say unto you, live on purpose in your purpose. #TeamNoFear

Day 27

TODAY'S WORD! Be encouraged today with each step you take to get closer to your dreams and goals. It is impossible to fail if you have faith in God and allow Him to lead and direct your path. Therefore, consider it joy when you have obstacles to overcome, hills to climb, and battles to fight. It only means you now have a chance to exercise your faith and show yourself how much you have learned and grown. Continue to move forward amid unbelief, doubt, criticism, and the lack of support. Know that if God is for you, that is more than the world against you. It is a guarantee that you will face opposition on this walk. The focus is not on how many times you fall; it is on what you do after you fall. What will you do? How will you react? What words will come out of your mouth? The answers to these questions will be the focus. **#TeamNoFear**

Day 28

TODAY'S WORD! You will continue to be defeated if you continue to speak defeat. You will continue to be broke if you continue to talk broken messages. You will continue to be sick if you speak sickness. Life and death are in the power of the tongue. Words can change your life and your way of thinking, good or bad. Consider the type of conversations that are being spoken around you. What is the message in these discussions? Be on guard and stay alert to what kind of seeds you allow to grow in your garden. How can you expect God to move in your life when you continue to speak that which is outside of his will? Not to mention what your actions are saying! Faith moves God's hand, and your words and actions show him that you agree with him. So be mindful of the words that come out of your mouth for your praise belong to God. Don't believe that it's just a song. What is the message? And remember there is a reaction to every action that you make. So, think before you sink. **#TeamNoFear**

Day 29
TODAY'S WORD! Never look at where you are but focus on where you are going. If you begin to focus on where you are, you may become distracted and wasting a lot of time. If you begin to focus on

where you are, you may become discouraged, and seeds of doubt may start to take root and grow. Have a vision and a plan, as well as dreams, goals, and a strategy in place to get there. If you don't have the least of these in place, you are sitting and spinning your wheels without forwarding motion. So, start with your vision, begin to see it, then, after that, begin to speak it and to work it. Faith without works is dead, and a vision without works has no promise. Today, focus on where you're going and remember the joy is in the journey. So never give up and never give in. **#TeamNoFear**

Day 30

TODAY'S WORD! Greetings, my brothers and sisters in the Lord. Keep in mind that trials come to make you strong. So why do you complain when they come? Have you so easily forgotten God's track record? Has his word fallen by the wayside in your life? Have what you seen with your eyes or felt in your body caused you to doubt God? He is the same yesterday, today, and forever and his Word will not come back to him void. I dare you to continue to confess God's Word and worship him in the middle of your storm and trial. Continue to stand and press on towards the mark despite adversity. You must refuse to give in or give up until you see change; this is the way of the faithful and the path to victory. So, choose this day to remember how far God has brought you. Lean not to your understanding but acknowledge Him in all your ways, and he will direct your path. **#TeamNoFear**

Day 31
TODAY'S WORD! It is a guarantee that you will face hardships in this life. But the focus should not be on the situation at hand but more so on your reaction. How will you react? What words will come out of your mouth? You see, everything in this life changes. The only thing you have that remains consistent and will never change or fail is GOD'S WORD. You must learn to continue forward and confess God's Word every step of the way no matter what you may face. If it rains, thank God that your seeds will be watered and soon you will be reaping a harvest. When you are walking with God, you should know

more than you did before you started walking with him. You will be given insight, wisdom, direction, and guidance to any and every situation you face. How can you make progress if you don't allow change to take place? How can you expect change if you continue thinking and speaking the old way? Be transformed by the renewing of your mind, and you will transform your life. #TeamNoFear

Day 32

TODAY'S WORD! Are the words coming out of your mouth hindering your progress? You see, words are like seeds; they are planted in your mind, and soon they will begin to grow. Consider the effects that weeds have on a beautiful garden, despite your best intentions. Plant the best seeds to grow the most beautiful flowers the eyes have ever seen. But if you allow weeds to grow, they will grow with the intent to destroy all your hard work. There is no compassion or unforgiveness in all their efforts to create havoc. If you allow them to take root and grow, it will take you longer for you to get rid of them then it took you to plant your garden. Life and death are in the power

31

of the tongue, and you choose what to speak. Never allow your circumstances or situations to dictate how you feel or what comes out of your mouth. You have a vital garden to protect where your dreams and goals are planted. #TeamNoFear

Day 33

TODAY'S WORD! Hello Christian, how are you? Wait, let me guess, you are blessed and highly favor. You are good and getting better, above and not beneath, etc., etc. Yet, I am in need, and you pass me by every day in front of the liquor store. You see me at the gas station and along the freeway, and yet you don't lend a helping hand or stop to pray for me. I understand that you are very busy and have many things to do. Maybe you are running late for a meeting or work. Maybe your favorite TV show is on, and you have already missed the first 10 minutes. I had a bible once and read in it that you have been put in place to lend and not borrow. I also know that God has given you the power to break the strongholds of poverty and addiction. He has blessed you according to his riches and glory, and I understand that if we touch and agree, he will do whatever it is that we ask. I could be mistaken about God's Word, or I could just mistake you for a Christian. Either way, I will continue to be patient and trust in the Lord of my salvation. **#TeamNoFear**

Day 34

TODAY'S WORD! Many of us forget who God is and what he is capable of when we face hardships. We allow words of defeat and unbelief to come out of our mouth. Our eyes see our situation, and our small minds try to see a way through it. But, do not forget that his ways are not our ways and His thoughts are not our thoughts. If you begin to give God praise and worship, no matter what you're in or where you at, you will begin to experience indescribable peace and reinsurance. You must be pushed out of your comfort zone to experience God's awesome power, or you will feel as if you can do it on your own. God takes over when you're not capable, but it is your faith that moves his hand. Your faith and the works of your hands will bring God's power and the awesome ability of his spirit. However, your words can hinder any progress that is about to take place. So, keep that in mind next time you choose to open your mouth and speak. Standing in agreement with God and his word, no matter the situation, is always a guaranteed VICTORY. **#TeamNoFear**

Day 35

TODAY'S WORD! What do you expect God to do while you sit back and do nothing? How can you expect your seeds to grow if you don't till the ground and plant your seed? Talking and running your mouth is not enough, and saying I am going to do this, and I am going to do that will get you nowhere. Faith without works is dead; there MUST be action on your behalf. How much effort are you putting forth in the fulfillment of your dreams and goals? God will help you by giving you favor, opening doors, and confusing your enemies who want you to fail. But he is NOT going just to take over so you can just sit back and relax. A child of God is willing to stand when everyone else wants to sit. A child of God will continue to press forward when everyone else wants to give up. A child of God will trust that victory is already given, so they will be glad to go into battle. So, I say unto you, get up and get moving. Stop complaining about where you are and focus on where you are going. **#TeamNoFear**

Day 36

TODAY'S WORD! What do your conversation and the words you speak say about you? What type of message are you conveying? If I were deaf, how would people describe your character? What type of person would people say you are? Would they say that you are a child of God, or would they say you never know what to expect from him or her? It's simple if I wanted a Big Mac, where would I go? If I wanted a Whopper, where would I go? You already know what to expect and where to get it. Your words and your actions are a HUGE part of who you are and, at times, can speak louder than your mouth ever could. So, check what you do and what you say, because it just may be the reason for the drama in your life. To move forward in God, sometimes you just need to SHUT UP and listen to what the spirit is saying. Open your heart to receive what God is trying to do in your life. **#TeamNoFear**

Day 37

TODAY'S WORD! What if you had 24hrs to live? What would you do? Where would you go? What would be your final words to your family and friends? The truth is that no one knows the day or hour of their death. So, settle your quarrels quickly, correct your wrongdoings, and forgive those who have hurt you. Many people walk around with hate and unforgiveness in their hearts, carrying this to the grave and never having the chance to make things right. Why carry something around that hinders you? You hear "Life Is Short" all the time, but many people take this truth for granted. You can tell by the way they live and how they act and treat others. Love while you can! Forgive while you can! The clock is ticking, and the days are getting shorter. Let not the chance to make your wrongs right. **#TeamNoFear**

Day 38

TODAY'S WORD Next time you choose to complain about your situation, consider those who wish to have the use of their limbs. Some hope that they could see the birds fly through the sky and the beautiful flowers that grow in the fields. Success is not based on how many accumulated material possessions that you have, the size of your home, or the amount of money in your bank account. Material things soon fade away, houses burn down, and money will come and go like the wind. Therefore, be thankful for those things that man cannot give nor can take away. Enjoy the sunshine, dance in the rain, and lift your hands to give God. He deserves all the glory and praise for both, now and forever. **#TeamNoFear**

Day 39

TODAY'S WORD! Do you have to be right all the time? If you are right 100% of the time, how can you learn anything? Most people fail to realize that you learn so much more when you watch and listen. Your job is not to convince people of anything but to plant seeds. God will bring the rain, and the seeds will grow, and God will teach the lesson. Be careful not to waste your time and energy on useless nonsense that will never bear good fruit. When you labor, do it with good intentions and a heart filled with love and compassion. Lend a helping hand whenever possible and let your actions speak for themselves so that the Lord of our salvation may be glorified. Trust in the Lord and lean not to your understanding, for he will give you instructions on the task at hand so that victory will be in your favor. May your ears be unplugged that you may hear. May your eyes be opened that you may see, and may your heart be receptive that you may receive today's word. #TeamNoFear

Day 40

TODAY'S WORD! Many people speak of faith but have a distorted view of what faith is and how it works. Faith works hand and hand with actions and patience. It involves being consistent and persistent in everything you do. The words you allow to come out of your mouth may hinder your work altogether. Those words, if spoken negatively, can distort your thinking, planting seeds of doubt, and growing unbelief. You should trust God every step of the way, no matter what your circumstances and situations may present. Making a choice to continue to move forward and having faith with actions is the key to your breakthrough and success. Refuse to give in or give up! The mindset and attitude to be unwilling to quit in the face of being outnumbered or overwhelmed is a must for every CHILD OF GOD. #TeamNoFear

Day 41

TODAY'S WORD! A light in a dark room is always helpful even if that light is not as bright as other lights you may have seen. Let your light shine, because there are many people lost and walking around in the dark, and without your light, they will remain lost. Give hope to the hopeless and food to the hungry. Never pass up a chance to speak a kind word or to lend a helping hand. TURN ON YOUR LIGHT! If you are in a position to lend, do so without a hidden agenda. Love your fellow brothers and sisters, pray for them and stand with them in their time of need. Give thanks for the small things, for these things are the foundation of life. TURN ON YOUR LIGHT! Always look for the opportunity to be a blessing to someone. Never complain about the rain, because without it, your seeds would wither and die. Rejoice when you wake up for this is a new day, and you will see new things. So, TURN ON YOUR LIGHT so that someone else may see. #TeamNoFear

Day 42
TODAY'S WORD! God has given you everything you need to reach greater heights. The problem is you don't want to let go of the things that are holding you back. Consider this, you have a brand new vehicle, but it has four flat tires; however, God has given you four brand new tires full of air. Here is the problem YOU DON'T WANT TO GET DIRTY AND CHANGE THE TIRES! You must press and seek out the things of God. You must be willing to surrender to his plan for your life. God is not going to override your brain and take away your option to choose. You must make a committed decision and follow through with your part. You must be consistent and persistent in every effort you put forth to achieve success. So, tell someone today. GET DIRTY! #TeamNoFear

Day 43

TODAY'S WORD! Why complain? What good will it do? Know that brighter days are ahead only for those who choose to keep walking. You may stumble. You may fall. You may come short but know if you choose to continue to move forward, in faith, God will give you the victory. There is no victory in giving up. There is no harvest if no seeds are planted. There is no faith without action, so choosing to do nothing is a plan for guaranteed failure. You have a part to play, and your part is to take God's Word at face value and step out on faith. Choosing not to step out will keep you in the same place with no forward motion. No forward motion means no progress to get from point A to point B, so; YOU MUST MOVE! It is not the time to doubt or be afraid. You should know that greater is he that is in you than he that is in the world. Proclaim and confess I can do ALL THINGS through Christ who strengthens me and begin to move without hesitation. #TeamNoFear

Day 44

TODAY'S WORD! There will be many who will quit and give up before they reach their goal; however, we will not, for our faith will help us to continue. There will be many that will fall by the waist side for the days will get dark, and the hours will get longer, but we will not for God walks with us. #TeamNoFear

Day 45

TODAY'S WORD! What is your purpose for being here? Why were you allowed to live one more day? You have just taken another breath, and your heart has just beat again. There is a reason and a purpose you were born who you are, and it's so awesome that there is only one of you. So, why on earth would you want to look like what the world says you should look? Society would have you to kill your image and deface your beauty. They want you to forget who you are all together and dance to the beat of their music. They want you to sing praises and thank them for entertaining you with foolishness and nonsense. They want all of your time and attention to be spent on them and the things they provide. The fact is that you are made in the image and likeness of God, and you are beautiful and wonderfully made. Not to mention that, but you are an heir to the throne and a child of the highest. All of your praise and worship belong to God, for he is a jealous God. Know who you are and whose you are for the world is trying to kill you. **#TeamNoFear**

Day 46

TODAY'S WORD! Don't think for one minute that God can't use you for his glory. I don't care where or who you are; God can work wonders. No matter how many times you have fallen or failed at making the right decisions. If you completely surrender and commit your life to him, he will give you an indescribable peace and joy that surpasses all worldly understanding. He will break your addictions and sever all unproductive relationships. He will give you staying power through his spirit and will lift you in your time of need. He will cause all your enemies to be a help instead of a hindrance. He will deliver you from sin and death and bring you into everlasting life.

He will cause your tears to water the many seeds you have sown. He will make your path straight and smooth giving you guidance and direction every step of the way. He is AWESOME and unable to fail! #TeamNoFear

Day 47

TODAY'S WORD! Better days are ahead if you choose to continue to move forward. The sun rises, and fall seasons come and go, but God's Word will always remain the same. For he is the same yesterday, today, and forever so, rejoice and give thanks. Change has to happen for you to grow, so don't reject it, be encouraged, and move forward in your faith in God. Consider a caterpillar whose life, in the beginning, consists of only crawling and eating leaves, not only that, but to some, as far as looks, it is not a sight to behold. Soon that same caterpillar will enter a cocoon and be completely transformed. It will go from crawling to flying, and people will admire its beauty so much that they get its image tattooed on their bodies. Remember, it was just a plain unattractive leaf- eating caterpillar that no one paid any attention to. Still, it went from crawling to flying (CHANGE), from a caterpillar to a butterfly (CHANGE), and from undesirable to desirable (CHANGE). You should continue to stand and walk in faith with God, and a CHANGE for the better will happen. **#TeamNoFear**

Day 48
TODAY'S WORD! Why complain? Know that brighter days are ahead only for those who choose to keep walking. You may stumble, you may fall, you may come short, but know if you choose to continue to move forward in faith, God will give you the victory. There is no victory in giving up and no harvest with no seeds planted. There is no faith without action, so choosing to do nothing is a plan for guaranteed failure. You have a part to play your part is to take God's Word at face value and then step out on faith. Choosing not to step out will keep you in the same place with no forward motion. And no forward motion means no progress to get from point A to point B. YOU MUST MOVE! Now is not the time to doubt or be afraid. Know that greater is he

that is in you than he that is in the world. Proclaim and confess I can do ALL THINGS through Christ who strengthens me and begin to move without hesitation. **#TeamNoFear**

Day 49

TODAY'S WORD! See yourself as God sees you, and you will never have to worry about what other people see or think. God knows you, and he knows the road you have walked. He knows your trials and tribulations and has seen all your dark nights. Do not let anyone tell you that you're not worthy enough or eligible to receive his grace, mercy, and salvation. For God so loved the world that he gave his only begotten Son, and salvation is available for those who will receive it. Know that you are delivered and set free from every chain of the enemy. Know that God can wipe every tear from your eyes and bring you into his perfect will that you may fulfill your destiny and purpose. It is up to you to completely commit and submit to God's will and his plan for your life. By doing so, you will experience the awesome transforming power of the word of God, which can make all the difference in the world. Therefore, believe and receive all that is available to you if you choose. **#TeamNoFear**

Day 50

TODAY'S WORD! There are two types of people -- those who know of God and those who know God. You can tell the difference by the fruit they bear, conversations they have, and by their actions. These three characteristics are tell-tell signs of which type of person you are dealing with. One will stand and continue to confess the word of God amid hardships no matter what the situation looks like. However, the other will allow words to come out of their mouth that will make the hardship look bigger than God. One will continue to say, but God said, and the other will quote a line from a movie or a verse from a song. One will have peace during the storm, looking forward to the rain. And the other will quickly run into the house to avoid getting wet. One will know that at times you must walk alone, and the other will complain because there is no one else around. One will cross the red sea, and the other will stay on dry land. Knowing *of* God does not give you the ability to get free from sin and death, but you now have his Holy Spirit on the inside, and that is the ability to overcome all things. There is a difference between knowing of something/someone and believing. #TeamNoFear

Day 51

TODAY'S WORD! If you find yourself feeling depressed, stressed out, and bound by the cares of this world, just begin to lift your hands and praise God, thanking him for your current circumstance. I know you may hear this a lot, "just thank and praise God," but I assure you that if you take this to heart, there will be a change. Faith in who God is and action on your part is the only way to get results. Don't pray for anything in particular just begin to thank him for being God. Watch the worries begin to fade away, and you will begin to feel restored with a new joy and a new hope. You see, many of us allow the cares of this world to appear as if they are bigger and greater than God. When, in fact, they are only temporary stops along the way to something far greater.

Remember, if there is no action, there is no change. Simply speaking, words is not enough. Get up and do something! **#TeamNoFear**

Day 52
TODAY'S WORD! Seasons change, and days continue to pass by as time keeps moving forward. But God remains the same yesterday, today, and forever. If you continue to stand in faith and on his Word, you will receive all that has been promised. How can there be progress with no forward motion? How is it possible for a rose to grow with no water? Continue to step out on faith and move forward, allowing God to water the seeds that you have planted. You must understand that there is a requirement for work on your behalf, so go till the ground and plant your seed. Commit time to study and pray so that you will begin to produce fruit and glorify God. Guard your heart and mind so that seeds of doubt and unbelief won't have a chance to take root. Surrender your mouth to the will of God and may the words that exit be those of encouragement, edification, and praise daily. Today is the day to go to

49

work! #TeamNoFear

Day 53

TODAY'S WORD! How can you expect God to
work miracles and move mountains on your behalf
and think that there is nothing required on your end?
The hand of God moves on your behalf according to
your faith. Your faith moves the hand of God
according to your works. For faith without works is
dead! Do not expect anything to happen or change
sitting down, and doing nothing, because you are just
wasting your time. Consider the children of Israel,
and they saw many miracles that God perform once
they left Egypt and begin their journey to the
promised land. Once they left, they had no choice
but to depend on God to protect and provide for
them. For you to experience the awesome
transforming power of God, faith and action are
required on your part. You must seek to find it! You
must knock for the door to be open! You must ask to
receive it! You, you, you must do, do, do, and stop
sitting on the sidelines waiting on God when he is
waiting on you. #TeamNoFear

Day 54

TODAY'S WORD! Hold fast and be encouraged for our God is awesome in all his ways and know that he will never leave you nor forsake you. Maintain the course and continue to stand under consistent pressure for if you faint not; great is your reward. Don't allow your circumstances and situations to dictate your outcome. Never allow words of doubt and defeat to exit your mouth. Be careful choosing what you allow to entertain you, for our enemy looks to plant seeds of destruction. Continue to meditate on the word of God, so in your dark nights, your light may continue to shine. Give thanks in every way and every season so that you may continue to move forward. Be ready and on guard for our enemy is circling the camp, looking for the lost. Fully commit to God's plan for your life so that in all things, you will know that there is purpose. Faith without works is dead, so continue to work that your faith may be alive. Look to be a blessing, for there are many wounded natural and spiritually. May these words fall on good ground in your heart, taking root and bringing forth one hundred-fold. May they also

51

encourage you to continue to move forward that you may fulfill your purpose. **#TeamNoFear**

Day 55

TODAY'S WORD! Be encouraged today and encourage someone else. Your problems may seem as big as a mountain, BUT GOD IS BIGGER. Know that if you completely put your trust in God, he will make a way out of no way. He will turn your mountain into a hill, and if you continue to stand on his word, he will then turn that hill into a bump. But this only happens with forwarding motion in faith on your part, for faith without works is dead. So, if you are standing at the foot of your mountain today, be encouraged. We all must walk our path in life, and there will be mountains, hills, and bumps along the way. Know that no matter what you face, our God is more than able to take you through it. Stand in faith, speak the word, and continue to move forward to victory. You may fall but GET BACK UP! You may slip but GET A GRIP! You may want to give up but ENDURE TO THE END! And watch God turn your journey into a wonderful experience that you wouldn't trade for the world. **#TeamNoFear**

Day 56

TODAY'S WORD! How can your faith grow
without hardships? Many people pray, Lord, I want
to be closer to you, and I want your will for my life.
But the minute they see the sign of trouble, they
shout Lord deliver me A.S.A.P., please Father God.
Many are like baby birds afraid to leave the nest, but
the day will come when you will be pushed out of
the comfort of the nest. You have been given wings
to fly but rather walk. You have been given legs to
run but rather crawl. God has given you everything
you need to continue forward, but you must step out
on faith, which requires action on your part. The
word of God, spoken from your mouth, and the no
hesitation to action attitude is the key to victory. You
must learn to trust God no matter where he has you
right now. Know that if you allow him to complete
his work in you, through patience, you will see his
hand move in a mighty way. Therefore, give him
praise in the middle of the storm. Shout glory
hallelujah, while dancing in the rain, for you know

that he holds all power, and he is working in your favor. **#TeamNoFear**

Day 57

TODAY'S WORD! For there is no other name given among men, by which we must be saved, other than the name of JESUS, who is our freedom and salvation. There is a war within all of us between the spirit and the flesh. You must choose which side you will continue to strengthen and to build. For those of you who think that music, television, and movies do not influence you or your spiritual growth, you are sadly mistaken. Be careful what you allow for entertaining you, for our enemy is strategic in his plan of attack and relentless in his efforts to mislead as many souls as possible. For we wrestle not against flesh and blood, Therefore, stay prepared, and aware, fully dressed for battle. You get out of it what you put into it; thus, you reap what you sow. And many times, chaos and confusion show up in our lives because of the seeds we have planted ourselves. Also, because of the words, we allow them to exit from our mouths. Therefore, plant seeds that will bear good fruit and speak words that will bring strength. May you make the choices that will bring you the victory and help you fulfill your purpose. **#TeamNoFear**

Day 58
TODAY'S WORD! Many people desire to have millions of dollars, to live in mansions with yachts, and have vacation homes across the world. Drive expensive cars and wear the latest fashion in jewelry and clothing. You can obtain all these things and still not have joy in your life. Would you trade your eyesight for all these things? Would you give up your legs for all of these things? How about your health, would you trade it? When everything is put into perspective, these things are not so important after all. Albeit, people do everything in their power to obtain as many of these things as possible. These things are temporary and will fade away just as the sun sets with each day. Be grateful for your health above all things. Rejoice in the fact that everlasting life awaits those who have accepted Jesus Christ as their personal Lord and Savior. Seek first the kingdom of God, and all of these things will be given to you. Make the necessary

changes today. **#TeamNoFear**

Day 59

TODAY'S WORD! Don't just hear these words but listen to them and understand them. When a warrior gets tired and frustrated, they consider quitting and giving up every day from the many battles that are fought. You are a spirit in a body that is made of flesh, so it is normal to feel this way. The spirit is willing, but the flesh is weak. The question is, what do you choose to do, and how do you react to these feelings? What separates those who don't get stronger and those who do is the decision to disregard those feelings and continue to move forward based on the word of God. If the spirit is willing and the flesh is weak, then you need to feed the willing spirit to get stronger. You wouldn't feed McDonald's to a 3-month- old baby, would you? Why not? What you feed your spirit is essential to your success to move forward in the things of God. So, seek those things which are eternal and everlasting, so that you may fulfill your purpose and destiny. **#TeamNoFear**

Day 60

TODAY'S WORD! Understanding what you are praying and asking God for will give you much clarity in situations you face daily. Consider this, you pray and ask God for patience; he doesn't just drop patience in your lap. He puts you in situations to develop your patience and, in turn, strengthens your faith and helps you grow. You want grace and mercy, so people come into your life for you to show them grace and mercy. Like the person who cut you off on the freeway or the person who took the parking spot, you had your eye on. Maybe it's the person who hasn't paid you back that money they borrowed. Here is your chance to have patience and show them grace and mercy. Do you just forget about your prayer and allow the enemy to use you? Have you considered the prayers you have been praying for? Why is God so small when it comes time for you to step out on faith? When all is well and good, you smile, but as soon as you see storm clouds, you run and take cover. God is able, but are you? God is willing, but are you? Watch what you pray for because you just might have to do some work you are not ready for. **#TeamNoFear**

Day 61
TODAY'S WORD! We all have fallen short at some time or another, but that doesn't change who God is. He is still able to pick you up and place your feet on solid ground. He is still able to take all the mistakes you have made and transform your life into a living testimony, offering hope to those who are lost in the darkness. For we are all sinners saved by grace, and it is because of his loving grace and mercy that we can continue this walk of faith. Lean not to your own understanding but acknowledge God in all your ways, and he will direct your path. Never cause your brother or sister to fall, but instead encourage them to keep their faith in our God, for he is awesome in all his ways. We all have hills to climb and giants to fight along the path we walk but know that the victory is given to those who faint not. Be encouraged and know that our God can do all things; however, he cannot fail, and you can do all things through Christ who strengthens you. Continue to move forward and look to be a blessing whenever possible. Brothers and sisters fighting together will accomplish more than

fighting one another ever will. Therefore, stand in faith and unity, offering praises unto our God on one accord. Watch the miraculous working power of our Lord and Savior be manifested throughout the land. #TeamNoFear

Day 62

TODAY'S WORD! Will you trust God? Many people will respond in the affirmative. However, when you are confronted with trials and tribulations, such as losing your money, becoming ill, losing a loved one, or your home, then will you still trust God? If so, why worry? Why allow the temporary things of this world to snatch your faith away? Why allow circumstances and people to cause you to doubt God's Word? Why allow rumors and words to plant seeds of destruction to crack your very foundation? The storm will come, but what will you do? How will you react? What words are coming out of your mouth? Either trust God all the way or choose not to go forward. Faith requires action, and you must press on to obtain your breakthrough. No fight is won without effort, and there is no victory without a war. Choose this day not to give up or give in, and you will see God do something amazing in your life. #TeamNoFear

Day 63

TODAY'S WORD! What good is it to read the bible (God's Word) and not apply it to your life? How do you help yourself by speaking words of doubt and unbelief? How is your spirit man strengthen by singing songs which consist of sex, money, and drugs? To whom do you sing praises to? Must we continue to go over the same lesson and around the same bush again? What you allow to entertain you will have an impact on your life. Why not just go to the gas station and fill your tank up at the kerosene pump? You cannot continue to plant weeds and expect to get flowers. Have you listened to the words that come out of your mouth? Have you paid attention to your attitude and your actions when faced with adversity? Set yourself up for victory by being ready and aware. By being willing and committed to God's purpose for your life. Watch, learn, and listen today; you might just be amazed at the benefits of the lesson being taught. #TeamNoFear

Day 64

TODAY'S WORD! There comes a time when you must make up your mind to walk in faith. Stand on God's Word and don't allow words of doubt and unbelief to exit your mouth. How can you fill a cup with water when the cup has a hole in the bottom? The words you choose to speak negative/positive will have an impact on your life. What you allow to entertain you will have an impact on your life, so choose wisely. Faith comes by hearing, so begin to build your faith by hearing that which is from God. His word is everlasting and shall never passaway and will give you strength in your time of weakness. How can you expect to win fighting a spiritual war in the flesh? Therefore, build up your spirit man by praying and reading the word of God. And begin to deprive your flesh of those things which are toxic to your walk with God. If you choose to surrender every area of your life to God and make a commitment to spend time in the word and prayer, you will begin to see change and progress. **#TeamNoFear**

Day 65

TODAY'S WORD! Insanity is doing the same thing over and over and expecting different results. How can you plant apple seeds and expect to get oranges? How can you continue to let words of negativity and conversations of gossip exit your mouth and expect positive things to happen? How can you stand on the word of God when you don't stand in it? How do you expect faith to be alive in your life when there are no works or actions on your behalf? God WILL NOT do everything for you; however, he will put you in a position to do for yourself. God wants you to have a Platinum black credit card with no credit limit. However, you settle for a bridge or EBT card because there is less work and minimum effort required to attain one of these. Stop being so lazy and ungrateful; instead, be active and humble. Look to be a blessing to someone whenever possible and lend a helping hand whenever there is a need. It's time to stand. You have been sitting on the sidelines long enough. Today you will be put in the starting lineup, so allow God to use you his purpose for your life. #TeamNoFear

Day 66

TODAY'S WORD! You are on your journey in this life, and it will be different from many other people's journeys. So, learn to enjoy your own life and stop trying to live someone else's life. God made you, and you are an original. Why in the world would you want to be like someone else? You are made perfect in the image and likeness of God. Smile BIG when you look in the mirror. Learn to love yourself and enjoy where God has you right now. Begin to see yourself as God sees you, and the only way to do that is to get in his word. Spending time in prayer is vital to the success of your journey. You wouldn't try to drive across the country with a half tank of gas, would you? The amount of gas would be vital to you making the trip. Therefore, take inventory of your own life and make the necessary changes. In doing so, you just may help others along the way. **#TeamNoFear**

Day 67

TODAY'S WORD! At some time or another, you will feel as if you have gone as far as you can go. That doesn't mean it's the end, nor does it mean you should give up either. It simply means that you need to begin to worship God for what he is about to do. God will step in at your breaking point, but you must allow him to do so. Your actions and your mouth may be a hindrance, so be sure to act in faith and check the words that come out of your mouth. You see, you can either do everything yourself, or you can allow God to help you. The choice is yours. Most people are defeated before they even get started by having a negative mindset and speaking words of doubt and unbelief. These are two guaranteed ways to failure. The keys to success are to submit and commit to God's plan and His will for your life. However, this cannot be done by wasting your time and energy on foolishness or nonsense. Standing firm in faith and giving time to prayer and reading the word will guarantee victory every single time without fail. Knowing what to do and doing it are two different things so, learn the difference to make a difference. **#TeamNoFear**

Day 68
TODAY'S WORD! Who told you that walking by

faith would be easy? Who told you that there wouldn't be any battles to fight? Who told you that you wouldn't lose "friends"? Who told you that you wouldn't have to walk alone sometimes? You have been misinformed walking by faith is not easy. There will be battles to fight, you will lose friends, and yes, sometimes you will have to walk alone. But it is in times like these that you experience the awesome power of God. Why complain about these things while you are walking with him? How long will it take for you to grow up? When will you truly commit to standing on his Word? Every day God is trying to tell or show you something. But you are so focused on your surroundings and situations that you miss it. Open your eyes, close your mouth, listen, and you just may receive what he has for you. There is a purpose and plan for your life, but you must submit and commit to God to receive it. Get focused on what's important and that which is everlasting because the time continues to pass with each day. #TeamNoFear

Day 69

TODAY'S WORD! STOP looking at where you are at and begin to focus on where you are going. Know that God has a plan for your life, but it will not happen by osmosis. It happens when your faith and actions become consistent and persistent when seeking out the things of God. I say this in LOVE, you are a child of the most high God, yet you are always complaining. The enemy has been fighting me all week. Would you all please pray for me? The enemy has been trying to keep me depressed and has been holding me back. Please pray for me. The enemy has attacked my body and my finances. Would you all please pray for me? He is doing what he is supposed to be doing, but are you? You are too busy running your mouth about what the enemy is doing that you have forgotten what God has DONE ALREADY. Listen, if you want to see an impact in your life, pray for someone else and watch what happens. Get up off your butt and put on the whole armor of God and begin to swing back, STOP just taking punches. Stop wasting your time and energy on nonsense. Give time to prayer and the word and less time to the TV. How do you expect to get stronger when all you do is feed the flesh? This is spiritual warfare, and your flesh cannot help you in any way. Sooner or later, you have got to fight on your own and stop looking for someone else to fight your battle. Grow up and begin training to become the great warrior who God has called you to be. #TeamNoFear

Day 70

TODAY'S WORD! If you choose not to continue forward, then there will be no growth. If you choose to allow what people say about you to affect your forward progress, then you will get nothing done. If you choose not to fight, then you will be defeated. If you choose not to plant your seeds, then they will wither away and die. THE CHOICE IS YOURS! So, stop waiting on God when he is waiting on you and stop blaming the enemy when it's your fault. The spirit is willing, but the flesh is weak. Get fully dressed and prepare for battle. Close your mouth, be quiet, and listen. For his ways are higher than our ways, and His thoughts are higher than our thoughts. Can you add one second to your life? Can you cause the sun to shine and the rain to fall? Can you cause the stars to shine bright in the midnight sky? What can you do? Well, do what you can and allow God to do what he does. WALK-IN FAITH! Trusting that God is able and faithful to bring that which he has spoken to pass. #TeamNoFear

Day 71

TODAY'S WORD! God will take your imperfections and make them perfect. Do not waste time on your flaws. Spend more time seeking, so that ALL things may be added unto you. Give less time to foolishness and nonsense, which does nothing but bring more foolishness and nonsense. Focus on that which strengthens the spirit, for this is a spiritual war, and your flesh cannot help you at all. What good will it do you to put water in the gas tank of your vehicle? How can you operate in faith without action? The words you speak and the choices you make are vital to your survival. So, don't take them lightly! Spending time in the presence of God before leaving the house is a sure way to ensure victory. But if you

68

don't take the time to do this, then why complain because you chose to be lazy? You chose some useless television sitcom, which does not strengthen your spirit before you walk out the door. You are going to battle and making a decision like that is very foolish on your part. Get your instructions and battle plan from God before leaving the house. **#TeamNoFear**

Day 72

TODAY'S WORD! What do the words you speak say about you? What does your conversation say about your character? Words are mighty and can be used to build someone up or tear someone down. Consider that God spoke the world into existence and that life and death are in the power of the tongue. So, the question is, what type of words are coming out of your mouth? Are your conversations building up or tearing down someone? Are they helping or hindering someone? If you choose to speak words of defeat, you will be defeated. If you continue to say my sinuses and my arthritis, they will continue to be yours. You must start by the renewing of your mind and do this by reading the word. Begin to change the words that come out of your mouth. If you choose to do nothing, you will get nothing. No results! No breakthrough! No forward motion! No healing! No Deliverance! Don't continue to allow your words to stop you from growing. **#TeamNoFear**

Day 73

TODAY'S WORD! Be encouraged today for our God is God, and he can turn your situation around. You must press in with prayer and stand on faith. Without doing these two essential things, you can't expect God to move on your behalf. What are you confessing? What are you spending your time doing? Are you confessing what the enemy said? Are you doing that which is outside the will of God? Talk is cheap, and nothing gets done without action on your behalf. When you should be lending a hand, are you looking for a handout? When you should be standing over your enemies, are you submitting to them.? When will you say enough is enough and begin to walk in the power and authority that God has given you? For greater is he that is in you than he that is in the world. You can do all things through Christ who strengthens you. Make this your confession daily according to the word of God. So, stop whining and start winning because today is your day. #TeamNoFear

Day 74
TODAY'S WORD! God doesn't change based on how you feel, and he doesn't move based on how your day is going. God moves according to your faith, and he moves according to you, acting on that faith. Many people are waiting on God, but the reality is he is waiting for them. Your seed must be in the ground when the rain comes, or you can expect nothing. You must be prepared and dressed for battle when the enemy comes, or you can expect no victory. So, the question is who or what are you waiting on? Time doesn't wait; neither does the day, so stop complaining and waiting for the perfect time to act on faith. You must realize that faith requires action on your part, for you to move. Get up, get out, and do something now! **#TeamNoFear**

Day 75
TODAY'S WORD! Tests and trials come to make you strong; however, along with strength, you can

also gain knowledge and wisdom. Knowing that they are a benefit to you, why do you complain? God the same God, even amid hardships! An athlete cannot compete in competition without intense training. A bird cannot hatch from an egg and begin fly immediately. However, it isn't until the athlete trains, or the bird overcomes its fear of falling that they begin to move towards their purpose. Know that greater is he that is in you than he that is in the world. You can do all things through Christ who strengthens you. For God has not given you the spirit of fear, so step out on faith and show your trials that your faith in God is bigger. Stop complaining and begin to walk in faith, speaking according to the Word of God. Allow your actions to and endure your hardships, for, in the end, VICTORY is yours. **#TeamNoFear**

Day 76

TODAY'S WORD! God has forgiven you, so why haven't you forgiven yourself? Stop wasting so much time on your imperfections and spend more time with God in his word and prayer. Sometimes we focus on our flaws so much that we accomplish nothing. Many people throughout the Bible were far from perfect, but they had faith in God and his word with the commitment to continue moving forward for God to use them to do great things. He wants to use you, but you must make yourself available. Continuing to complain about where you are and what's going on will not get anything done. Each day requires that you commit to get better and do better. Be aware of how you invest your time and what you spend your time doing. You can plant the seed, but you cannot make it grow. Therefore, continue to plant as many seeds as possible, so when the rain comes, you will be dancing in it while everyone else is on the porch. #TeamNoFear

Day 77

TODAY'S WORD! Why waste so much of your time and energy on nonsense? Why allow your enemy to get you sidetracked with issues that are not important? How much longer will you continue to fall for the same old tricks? There comes the point and time in your walk with God when you just have to grow up. How is it possible to walk with the Lord for years and learn nothing? To receive what God has for you, a true commitment to act on the word in faith must take place. Not a continuous habit of just reading the word and doing what you want. How can you expect growth walking in the flesh? There is no victory for the flesh in a war that is spiritual. God is looking for a 100% commitment, not 99.9%. Jesus committed 100% to the will of the farther to the cross. No matter what he faced, he remained committed, and the whole time, he had you in mind. #TeamNoFear

Day 78

TODAY'S WORD! Your life is like a book; continue to read each chapter every day. Some chapters may be better than others but know that God is the author and finisher of our faith. If things are bad, they will soon be better. If you are in a storm, the clouds will soon clear, and the sun will shine if there are tears of sadness. They will soon be turned to joy and laughter. Know that God has not given up on you, so lift your head and stand. Make a committed decision to surrender to his will for your life. Begin to feed your spirit man the word of God so that the temptations of life won't overtake you so easily. Fix your face like flint and become unmovable in your faith. Combine action with your faith and watch God move on your behalf. Day by day, and page by page, things will get better. Failure is a choice only you can make, but failing is something that God can't do so, choose him instead. **#TeamNoFear**

Day 79

TODAY'S WORD! Are you in prison? A prison of unforgiveness could mean death for you spiritually and may just kill your dreams and goals. How can you expect God to forgive you if you are not willing to forgive others? Have you lost focus? Have you lost track of the enemy? For we wrestle not against flesh and blood, Therefore, stay prepared and aware fully dressed for battle. Not forgiving someone is like taking a shower in gasoline. If you and the person you have not forgiven get close to a flame, guess who burns up? YOU! Guess what type of arrows the enemy shoots at you? You see, you make yourself an easy target to hit, and holding unforgiveness in your heart has no benefit to you at all. How can you love

75

and not forgive? God first loved us; then, he forgave us. For God so loved the world that he gave his only begotten son. Jesus did his work first, and then he went to the cross for us. (Love & Forgiveness) they work for hand and hand like (Faith & Action). So today, forgive and forget that you may receive healing for your body and spirit. Walk out of the prison that has held you for years. The prison door has always been wide open, but unforgiveness has kept you imprisoned. Today forgive and walk out! **#TeamNoFear**

Day 80

TODAY'S WORD! Are you ungrateful? Many of us complain about the rain, and yet others pray that the drought ends. Many of us throw out perfectly good food, while others would be overly joyful for a piece of bread. Many of us have closets filled with clothes, yet some people have nothing to wear. Many of us complain about having to do something or be physical, yet there are people laid up in a hospital, hoping to one day walk in the sunlight again. Take inventory of your life and consider how much God has truly blessed you. Stop complaining and look to be a blessing to someone less fortunate. #TeamNoFear

Day 81

TODAY'S WORD! What are your motives behind your actions? Are your intentions honest and truthful? You may fool people, but it is impossible to fool God. For his ways are not our ways, neither are His thoughts our thoughts. To my fellow brothers and sisters in Christ, remain faithful to God and honest in all your actions. To those who are dishonest and deceitful, you will reap what you sow. Let not our enemy and his company of labors get you sidetracked from the task at hand. For in your time of distraction, many souls are being lost. Stay aware and on guard for our adversary is looking to advance. Let not words of hate and discouragement exit your mouth. At all times, be found encouraging and edifying the body of Christ. The hand is no good without the wrist, and the wrist is no good without the arm. So, let your light shine that it may glorify our God in heaven. Today look to build up! Look to encourage! Look to be a blessing! Look to help where there is a need! Do this so that the loss in this world may know that God and his people are at work. **#TeamNoFear**

Day 82

TODAY'S WORD! Stop looking for a blessing if you're not willing to be a blessing. Stop expecting people to stop lying on you and treating you unpleasant if you are not willing to get the ball rolling by doing the opposite. Why should people around you do better when you are not setting a good example? If you want to change, the first place you should look is in the mirror. Stop talking and start getting things done. No matter what you believe, faith without action equals nothing. Until you make a solid foundation with faith and action, you will not see any changes in your life. Simply stop talking about what you are going to do and do it. What are you spending most of your time doing now? Is what you're spending your time on going to benefit your spirit, or will it benefit your flesh? You cannot expect to win a marathon without being prepared. So today, start the change with you, and it will become contagious, affecting your life and everyone else around you. #TeamNoFear

Day 83
TODAY'S WORD! Focus on the task at hand and give no thought to negativity. Be thankful for reach day and lend a helping hand whenever possible. Know that God walks with you and at no time should you fear anything #TeamNoFear

Day 84
TODAY'S WORD! So, you say you want things to change, right? You pray that things would be different for you. The real question is, what will you do differently? If you continue to think the same way, you will continue to speak the same way. God's thoughts are higher than our thoughts, and His ways are higher than our ways. The renewing of your mind must transform you, and your mouth will begin to speak the word of God into your life. You see, the spirit is willing, but the flesh is weak so, there is no time to give in to weakness if you don't change. You continue to let the same people and things upset you

over and over. When will you grow up? If there is no time spent in prayer, and in the Word, there will be no change. For faith comes by hearing and hearing the word of God. Without faith, it is impossible to please him, so how then do you expect change to come from laziness? Today is the day to get real with yourself! #TeamNoFear

Day 85

TODAY'S WORD! To eliminate all confusion and misunderstanding, be honest and open with people upfront. You gain nothing trying to hide evil or dishonest intentions. God knows the heart of man, so; you will be judged accordingly. Do not think for a minute that you will escape. If the Holy Spirit dwells in you, why would you look to deceive your fellow brothers and sisters anyway? What do you hope to gain by doing so? You will reap what you sow, and if you sow deceit and dishonesty, it will spring up at a time when you are least likely to expect it. Walk in the spirit, operate in love, so that our Father in heaven may be glorified. Look to be a blessing and strengthen your fellow brothers and sisters, for there is a fierce battle with the passing of each day. The number of your hairs on your head has been counted, and time has no pause button. So, use your efforts to do that which is pleasing to God, and in due time you will be going home. #TeamNoFear

Day 86

TODAY'S WORD! Everyone has a season. When you plant an apple seed in the ground, you cannot control when it grows, how fast it grows, nor the size of the tree or the apples it produces. You can water the seed nurture at its most vulnerable state, protecting it from too much sun or pests that would love to eat it before it has the chance to produce apples. When the tree matures and begins to yield fruit, this is a great reward because of the apple pie, apple sauce, apple cider, apple jelly, etc. You must learn to remain focused on what's important and be patient, for, in due season, you will reap what you have sown. So, learn to protect your seed and give less time to foolishness and nonsense. Remain watchful and on guard for there are many pests out there. #TeamNoFear

Day 87

TODAY'S WORD! Having patience is a hard but valuable lesson to learn. If you can only learn to trust the Lord, no matter where you are, and never allow your mouth to utter words of complaining, you will be amazed at the things God will pull off. If his thoughts are not our thoughts and his ways are higher than ours, then why complain? If you acknowledge Him in all your ways, why not trust him to direct your path? Faith and action will move the hand of God, not complaining and unbelief. You can control what comes out of your mouth, so why not let those words be in alignment with God's Word? What good will it accomplish? How will it help you? Make up your mind to either trust him 100% or not at all. He is not a part-time God, and he isn't off on weekends. So, make up your mind to stand in faith and on his word, no matter where you are or what you may be facing. **#TeamNoFear**

Day 88

TODAY'S WORD! There is a season and time for all of us, so remain patient. There is a season to reap and a season to sow. There is a time to move and a time to remain still. However, no matter where you are or what you're going through, one thing remains consistent, and that's God's Word. Along with his word and your faith, no battle can't be won. No enemy will remain standing, and victory is yours for the taking. Jesus came to deliver, save and set free those who are bound by sin and death. However, you must choose to accept him as your personal Lord and Savior to receive this freedom. Victory over sin, death, and the grave cannot be yours unless you make a choice. There is no other name given among men, whereby we must be saved, but it is in the name of JESUS that all things are done. So, seek him to find salvation and everlasting life. **#TeamNoFear**

Day 89
TODAY'S WORD! Forgiveness is a mighty act, and to choose to do so will produce undeniable results in your life. You would be amazed at how many people are locked inside the prison of unforgiveness. Locked inside a prison that they have the key to and could free themselves at any time. However, because of

their hardened hearts and choosing to give in to the flesh, they remain locked up. They remain unproductive spiritually and carry around this weight, which hinders their progress from moving forward. The past is the past, and you cannot bring back yesterday so, why dwell in that place. What good will it bring you? Instead, you can choose to make better decisions and allow the Holy Spirit to show you how to heal. There is enough fighting with your enemies so, why fight with yourself. Commit to follow God at all costs, and unforgiveness will not have a cell waiting for you. **#TeamNoFear**

Day 90
TODAY'S WORD! Stop putting things off all the time and try to get done as much as possible each day. Procrastination kills the goals and dreams of people every second of the day. Fear tries to suffocate the very life and hope out of them before they even get started. In the pursuit of your dreams and goals, you may hear many NOs before you hear one YES, by all means, do not quit or give up. In the beginning, there may be what seems like a lack of support from family

and so-called friends, but by all means, keep moving forward. You may hear, "You can't do that" or "How are you going to get that done" or "That is going to take too long," and other such inquiries. When you hear questions like these, stop, turn around, look them in the face and say as loud as you possibly can "HUSH, IAM WORKING"! Put your faith in action today by standing on God's word, despite what your eyes see, or your mind tries to tell you. God has a plan for your life! Today, step out on faith and tell some of the people in your life "HUSH IAM WORKING"! #TeamNoFear

Day 91

TODAY'S WORD! You must be consistent and persistent in your walk with God, or you will hinder your progress. Taking your faith and applying God's Word is the recipe for success. The spirit is willing, but the flesh is weak. Stand when you want to sit and pray when you want to sleep. Begin to do the opposite of what your flesh wants. There is a war within you, and the side you feed the most becomes the strongest. There is work required on your behalf to see results. Don't just think things are going to happen magically because they will not. And don't deceive yourself by thinking God is going to do everything, because you are wrong again. Faith and action get God's reaction. So, what are you doing? Meditate on his word, begin to speak his word, and then act on his word. MEDITATE+SPEAK+ACT (REPEAT). **#TeamNoFear**

Day 92
TODAY'S WORD! What or who will you let come between you and God? What or who could be that important that you allow them to have that much of your time? Why look for God in times of trouble, after spending most of your time outside the presence of God? You give your praise to the world, as it gives you nothing back in return. You worship those who are being broadcast on your radio frequencies and televisions, as they walk the red carpet in confidence. Be not deceived, because our enemy is like the sugar in the sweetest candy. When enough of it gets in your system, it will cause catastrophic damage. Check the message, and in it, you will see the plan of chaos and

confusion. Why then do you support that which opposes the kingdom of God? You may be in this world, but not of this world. The renewing of your mind has transformed you. Let your time be spent with God and let your worship be given to him and him only. For there is no other name given among men, whereby we must be saved. **#TeamNoFear**

Reflections/Notes:

Reflections/Notes:

Reflections/Notes:

90

Reflections/Notes:

Day 93

TODAY'S WORD! Being prepared before leaving your home to go about your day is your responsibility, not God's. God will equip you with what you need to be victorious in your battles, but it is up to you to be prepared. So, if you're not prepared, get ready to be aggravated and frustrated. Get ready to be uncomfortable and annoyed by every little thing someone does. Circumstances and situations are consistent in everyday life, are you? Having the word of God at your disposal and not applying it to your life is ineffective and will bear no fruit. Stop always looking for a handout from God and begin to walk in faith that you may please him; so that others may see your light and glorify our Father in heaven. Today become the mighty warrior who defeats every enemy who opposes God's Word and his everlasting kingdom. Now is the time of faith and action! #TeamNoFear

Day 94

TODAY'S WORD! Stop beating yourself up when you make a mistake. Let's be clear there is a difference between a mistake and an addiction. There is also a difference between knowing what's right and wanting to do wrong. You are a spiritual being living in a body made of flesh, so there will be many mistakes made. It is not the mistakes that hinder your progress, but what you choose to do after them. Mistakes are learning, and growth opportunities meant to make us stronger and wiser than you are before. If you continue to make the same mistake over and over, it is no longer a mistake but addiction or just downright foolishness. It is imperative that you know the difference and adjusts your lifestyle accordingly. Time will not pause for you, nor will your enemies show you any mercy, so stay diligent in your pursuit to seek the Lord. Mistakes will be made, but keep in mind how important it is to make better decisions after them, or your life will be stuck on repeat with continuous failure. **#TeamNoFear**

Day 95
TODAY'S WORD! What do you expect God to do while you sit and do nothing? How can you expect a harvest when you haven't planted any seeds?

Believing in God is not enough! After all, the demons in hell believe in God. By accepting him as your personal Lord and Savior, while acting on faith, according to his word, is a different story. God does not move because you believe, but he moves because you have faith. You would not pray for a job, without ever applying for one, because that would not make sense, would it? Or maybe you're praying, Lord blesses me, but you never look to be a blessing. There MUST be action attached to your faith to get results. You must get off your butt, because sitting around crying, 'poor little old me, why is everyone out to get me?' The truth is you have only yourself to blame. Laziness and procrastination are two of the biggest problems that hinder your forward progress. The spirit is willing, but the flesh is weak, so make your adjustment accordingly. Sitting at a green light, waiting for it to turn red makes no sense. Open your eyes, unplug your ears, get off your butt and get some work done. **#TeamNoFear**

Day 96

TODAY'S WORD! Be careful not to get sidetracked by nonsense and foolishness. You have been given time, but it continues to tick away with each passing day. Continue to walk by faith for our God is God, and there is no other above him. Victory is given to those who faint not and who are in continuous pursuit of the Kingdom of God. The words you speak are vital to your survival, and your mindset is the foundation of your success. Speak that which God has spoken and be transformed by the renewing of your mind so that victory and success are guaranteed. The spirit is willing, but the flesh is weak; Therefore, build that which is willing, and that which is weak, let it fall to the wayside. Walk in the light. May you see the many snares of the enemy, but do not believe his words of doubt and unbelief. For our God is awesome, and his kingdom reigns forever and ever. #TeamNoFear

Day 97

TODAY'S WORD! Keep in mind that your life is just a vapor, and your time here on earth is short. How will you be remembered? What words will be whispered about you behind closed doors? What type of legacy will you leave, if any? The things we do here will be echoed in eternity. At all times, let your words be honest and your heart free from hate and strife. Let your intentions be clear and open so that there will be no confusion. Seek the will of God as if it was your lost child. Continue to press forward, that you may acquire purpose for your life. Live today as if it was your last and make amends with your fellow neighbors. For even the sun shines for a short time and then it sets. You have been given another day to make things right, so do so quickly, for the sun will soon set, and the moon will rise. Today is your day to get things in order. **#TeamNoFear**

Day 98

TODAY'S WORD! Harvesters get ready to reap the mighty. The rain is about to fall, and our seeds will bring forth a great harvest. God is going to increase your seed hundred-fold for Those who have sown and planted seeds. You have shown faithfulness over and over, and you have stood in faith in God's Word during your storms. God will cause many doors to open, and he will cause your enemies to be scattered abroad. He will cause every stumbling block set before you to be a steppingstone to your success. He will wipe away your tears and cause your heart to be filled with joy. God is moving behind the scenes on your behalf, so get ready because your time of blessings is at hand. Those who have sown and stood in faith, on God's Word, GET READY, the Lord of our Salvation is about to move in a mighty way. Step out and step up to receive it today, said the Lord of host! **#TeamNoFear**

Day 99

TODAY'S WORD! Brothers and Sisters in Christ don't just hear this but understand it. There are many people in need of food, money, and shelter, and you tell them, "I will pray for you" is not enough. Please understand that there is nothing wrong with praying for them. But if you can give them money or food, then do so. Doing this will meet their needs right then and there. "Don't be so spiritually minded that you're no earthly good," but do allow God to use you to be a blessing to someone else. What good will it do to hand a bible to someone who can't read? Instead, minister to them at your full capacity, physically and spiritually, allowing them to experience God's love for them. Faith with action is undeniable and unstoppable! **#TeamNoFear**

Day 100

TODAY'S WORD! During my storm, I will continue to give God praise. In the middle of my hardships, I will lift my hands and continue to give him glory. I know that his plan for me is good, and his love endures for all of eternity. I say yes and amen to his will and his purpose for my life. I will continue to be grateful for each step forward, and I will and forever be humble with every blessing. Lord continue to fill me with your joy for the joy of the Lord is my strength. In my times of trouble, make my path clear and straight. You are awesome, and your kingdom is everlasting; all truth and righteousness come from you. Magnify the name of the Lord countless times over, and may his grace and mercy find me in my time of need. **#TeamNoFear**

Day 101

TODAY'S WORD! Don't think for one minute that you can hide from God. You cannot hide yourself, your thoughts, or your motives, so it may be in your best interest, to be honest. Let your intentions be clear, and your words understood so that there is no confusion among yourselves. Hold to righteous and let go of that which will cause you to fall. Submit to God, and he will commit to you and allow your actions to be your faith according to the Word of God. Repent while the sun is still up, for when the moon comes, it will be too late. Seek the Kingdom of God, so that you may obtain that which is eternal. For your life is but a vapor, and the clock continues to tick as this fleshy vessel decays. So, focus on that which is willing and not that which is weak, so that you may obtain what is eternal. Continue to move forward in the things of our Lord. **#TeamNoFear**

Day 102

TODAY'S WORD! There is no other God like our God, who is awesome in all his ways. He spoke the world into existence and caused the sun and the moon to shine. He brings healing, where there is hurt and joy where there is sorrow. He brings life where there is death and hopes where there is hopelessness. Lift him and exalt his holy name for all of eternity. Marvel at his wonderful creations while being grateful for his love and forgiveness. He has made me glad, and I will forever rejoice and give his name all the praise and glory. If it had not been for the Lord, where would I be? Your praise crushes every problem, and your worship heals every wound. May the Lord of our salvation continue to move us forward. **#TeamNoFear**

Day 103

TODAY'S WORD! If you continue to do nothing, then nothing will continue to happen. Talking about what you want to accomplish and keeping that idea in your head will never get any physical work done. You can have a basket full of seeds, but until you work the ground and plant them in the dirt, you will not get the full benefits of those seeds. Eventually, they will wither up and die, taking their full potential with them. Never expect everyone to do everything while you sit back and daydream. If you are not willing to go without sleep and not willing to do the work, then be prepared to sit back and watch your dreams and goals die. Praying to God, and not having any action on your part will not bring results. Faith is action, and with no action, there is no reaction; it's that simple. So today, stop complaining and start doing, and God will start moving. **#TeamNoFear**

Day 104
TODAY'S WORD! How can you call out the enemy and not be prepared to fight? How can you not expect opposition from those who oppose the will of God? You cannot continue to play church and think that there is not a spiritual war that exists. You are a spiritual being in a fleshy body, and that body dies daily. However, that body can also cause you to doubt God's Word and his plan for your life. Therefore, you must continue to do that, which will strengthen the spirit. You do not allow the things you see, hear, and feel in this body to cause you to doubt that which is eternal. For the heavens and earth will pass away before God's Word will fail. Greater is he

that is in you than he that is in the world because you can do all things through Christ who strengthens you. But you must prepare and walk in faith standing on the Word of God, or the enemy will surely defeat you in every area of your life. **#TeamNoFear**

Day 105

TODAY'S WORD! Your goal is to keep your faith in God and trust that no matter what you may face, he has a plan for good for you. Faint not during your storms and hardships for our God is God. If you do something good for someone, do it because you expect nothing in return. Putting your faith in man, family, or friends, expecting them to do the right thing all the time, will soon prove to be disappointed. Your faith should always and forever be in God, and you should be expecting him to bless you. Don't set yourself up for failure by expecting a man to do right and never allow what happens to hinder your walk by acting out in the flesh. Good and evil comes out of the heart of man, but only good from the heart of God. Therefore, walk in the spirit and operate in it daily, so that you may have the advantage over your adversary. Disconnect yourself from foolishness and nonsense so that your judgment may not be distorted. #TeamNoFear

Day 106

TODAY'S WORD! Keep in mind no matter what you are going through or what you may be in right now, God's Word will never change. (God's Word doesn't change it changes things) Not knowing his word is like having a gun without bullets. How can you be effective in spiritual combat when you spend much of your time watching uselessness nonsense on TV? At the first sign of the enemy, you panic, and with one smart word or attitude from someone, you lose it. For we wrestle not against flesh and blood, and by your reaction, I can tell your judgment is cloudy. How long will it take you to mature? You will not grow an apple tree by planting orange seeds. Now is the time to refocus and regain your footing, for our enemy is circling the camp. **#TeamNoFear**

Day 107

TODAY'S WORD! As you breathe, remember God

blew into your nostrils the breath of life and man became a living soul. There is a purpose for your life, and it is not to just go through the motions. It is not to invest your time and energy in uselessness nonsense. It is not to be entertained by those who continuously preach a message of SEX, MONEY, and DRUGS from their television, music, and movie pulpits. What you may think is harmless entertainment is planting seeds of destruction. Be sure to look for a deeper meaning. However, in today's world, the message is clear. You are who or what you support. So, then what is your purpose? There are millions of brothers and sisters being slaughtered each second, physically and spiritually. There is a spirit of carelessness and death running rampant through our lands. God is calling a meeting, and that meeting is called prayer. Answer the called today, so that you may find your purpose and begin to walk in what God has for you. There are souls at stake and life of everlasting living, so get to that meeting. #TeamNoFear

Day 108

TODAY'S WORD! He is a miracle-working God and can do more than we can ever imagine. However, it is our work with the faith that gets his attention. Surrender all that you are to him and allow him to use you in a mighty way. Stop wasting your time and energy on nonsense that will do nothing but breed more nonsense. Stop allowing the devil to use your mouth to speak. Stop giving in to doubt and unbelief. Stop waiting for tomorrow to come to walk in your purpose. Stop passing the time with unproductive people. Stop falling for the same old foolishness. Put yourself on notice and say, "Self, this nonsense stops today!" When you think to *change*, speak *change*, and act on faith, the *change* will happen. #TeamNoFear

Day 109

TODAY'S WORD! To grow, you must step out on faith and take the word of God at face value. If there is no faith, there will be no growth. The words you allow to come out of your mouth must be words of faith. The renewing of your mind must transform you because believing just is not enough. The demons in hell believe. You must put action with your faith to move the hand of God. For without faith, it is impossible to please him. You must step out to move forward. So, you say you believe, but the question is, what are you doing with what you believe. How do you put your faith to work? You must not allow what you see with your eyes to hinder your faith in the word of God. We must learn to walk by faith and not by sight. We must learn to continue to speak words of faith and not those of doubt and unbelief. Continue to say to your circumstances what God said and act on his word every single time, no matter what you see or hear. **#TeamNoFear**

Day 110

TODAY'S WORD! My fellow brothers and sisters in Christ; I am afraid that we have lost focus on what the gospel of Jesus Christ came to accomplish. We have been blinded by the message of prosperity and worldly possessions. Having this as the foundation of your message and striving to obtain these things will result in emptiness and the true loss of love and life. The gospel came to provide Salvation, Love, Forgiveness, and to develop a mindset to serve. For God so loved the world that he gave his only begotten son that whosoever call upon the name of Jesus will be saved. And she shall bring forth a child, and you shall call his name Jesus for he will save his people from their sins. Therefore, first, seek the kingdom of God and his righteousness, and all these things will be added unto you. Plant your feet firmly in that which is eternal for this life will soon pass away. Look to serve and provide physical and spiritual strength to your fellow brothers and sisters, so that they may continue to move forward in the things that our Lord has called them to do. And above all, these hear, listen, and get understanding that these words may take root in your heart and bring forth a hundred-fold. #TeamNoFear

Day 111

TODAY'S WORD! Under no circumstances do you ever let the enemy steal your praise. For God dwells in the praises of his people, and most times, that is exactly where your breakthrough is located. If you can continue to give God praise, no matter the situation, you will begin to see just how awesome God is. His plan and his will must be priority number one in your life. Once you accept that, you will begin to walk in the direction of your purpose and destiny. The flesh will get you sidetracked and have you to direct your focus on that which is temporary. Losing focus is a waste of time for this life, and everything in it will pass away. However, God's kingdom and his Word will not, and this is the true- life we are meant to live. This life is a vapor over in a blink of an eye, but the kingdom of God is everlasting. The flesh is like a flower that withers away in the sun. However, the spirit is like the rain that falls from the sky and brings life to all. Therefore, walk in the spirit and commit to the will of God that you may find your purpose. **#TeamNoFear**

Day 112
TODAY'S WORD! Lord, may you find me in my time of need and give me the strength to overcome my hardships. I know that trials come to make me strong, and your grace and mercy endure forever. Let

your peace reign supreme, and your spirit provide liberty and freedom all the days of my life. I lean not to my understanding but acknowledge you in all my ways so that you may direct my path. For your ways are not my ways; neither are your thoughts, my thoughts. You know all and see all, for there is nothing impossible for you. Let your will be accomplished in every area of my life. I submit and commit to that which is of you to you. Glory and honor belong to you, and with each breath, I take to let it be a praise unto your holy name, for you are the truth amid lies and the peace during the chaos. Your kingdom is everlasting, and your word brings life to that which was dead. May you continue to move me forward in faith and guide me to my destiny and purpose. #TeamNoFear

Day 113

TODAY'S WORD! You will never see an eagle hanging out with a chicken, nor will you see them flying together. There is a tremendous power source on the inside of you, which is called the Holy Spirit. Many gifts and talents are lying dormant, waiting to be awakened to be used for God's glory. However, it will continue to be difficult if you keep hanging around chickens. Chickens become chicken nuggets, chicken wings, chicken sandwiches, etc., but eagles become state birds, monuments, protected species, and not to mention very effective hunters. Eagles fly alone, reaching heights many birds will never reach. They are constantly on the search and overcome some of the deadliest living creatures on earth. Chicken walk on the ground all day eating scraps thrown to them and wouldn't last a minute with some of the creatures the eagle encounters. So, eagle, today, stop wasting your time by hanging with chickens. #TeamNoFear

Day 114

TODAY'S WORD! Sometimes the hardest thing to do is to accept the will of God.

It is not hard for the spirit, but it is the flesh that makes it so hard for us. The spirit is willing, but the flesh is weak. Therefore, we must strive to walk in the spirit. Never wavering but trusting God's plan and His will for our lives and standing firm on his word and his promises despite the odds. Learning to accept his will when it seems to go against everything we want, or desire may be one of the hardest things you will ever have to do. But know that his plan for us is good and that he is faithful in all his ways. And there is nothing in heaven or on earth that is above him. Following the leading of the spirit requires us to give a deaf ear to the flesh, as this is the only way to guarantee our forward progress. May we all submit and commit to what God has for us all and may your walk with him be a testimony for others. #TeamNoFear

Day 115

TODAY'S WORD! Be fully persuaded in your faith so that when hardships and trials come, you do not easily waiver. Never consider giving in or giving up in the middle of the storm. Have a one-track mind and set it on acting on the word of God in the middle of the storm. When the wind blows, lift your hands with praise. When the rain falls, rejoice in the fact that your seeds are being watered, when the thunder rumbles and the lighting flashes, stand in awe of God's awesome power. Look for the lesson in everything you do and search for the eternal. Look to sow seeds whenever possible so that you may dance in the rain. Let your words be kind, for many may not have a full 24hrs. With every intention, be truthful and honest so that confusion will have no place to live. And may the Lord of our salvation continue to move us forward towards destiny and purpose. **#TeamNoFear**

Day 116

TODAY'S WORD! Change starts with you and the decision you make. Therefore, never take them lightly. The music you listen to, the movies you watch, and the people you choose to hang around all play a part. Spirits are trying to influence you every day, so be sure that you entertain the right ones. How many times must we go over the same lesson? Your song of praise belongs to God and him only! Be not deceived by the small things that cause big problems in the overall picture. Guard your heart and keep a watchful eye for our enemy is circling the camp. **#TeamNoFear**

Day 117

TODAY'S WORD! If you are willing to listen, God will discuss his plans with you just as he has done many times over. However, you must submit and commit to him, and be willing to let go of those things that may feel comfortable. You must be willing to deny what your eyes may see and what your flesh is telling you. You must walk in faith against all the odds and continue to confess the word of God in any situation. The path is straight and narrow; therefore, keep your feet firmly planted in the word of God. How can you understand or hear when your mouth is always moving? Sit still. Be quiet. Listen to what God has to say concerning your destiny and purpose.
#TeamNoFear

Day 118

TODAY'S WORD! Listen if you pray for patience because it doesn't just fall in your lap. God puts you in situations that will cause you to be patient. Likewise, if you pray for grace and mercy, he puts you in a position to show someone else grace and mercy, so every day with every situation, be watchful and pay very close attention. You must be looking for confirmation to your prayers with expectations and faith that God has already answered them. Once God has placed you in the position to have your prayers confirmed, then to allow your flesh, people, or circumstance to move you out of that position is like jumping out of a plane without a parachute. Sooner or later, you will hit the ground. OUCH! You will find yourself broken, bruised, and hurt, while possibly blaming God and everyone else when the blame is all yours. After all, it was your prayer, so stay out of the kitchen if you can't cook or are not willing to learn. This Christian walk is not for the lazy or the prideful, but for those who are willing to completely submit and commit to God's plan for their lives under any circumstance. Therefore, be mindful when you pray and choose your words carefully. **#TeamNoFear**

Day 119
TODAY'S WORD! If you allow yourself to be surrounded by negative people and negative things, sooner or later, you will get infected. You will start having symptoms after planting those things in your

life via people, television, music, and movies. Be transformed by the renewing of your mind, so that you will be able to see your enemy's plan. Guard your heart so that these seeds will have no place to grow. Sharpen your sword so that when you swing it, the very air you breathe is cut. There is no mercy for those who opposed God and look to take down his kingdom. So, discern yourself accordingly that you may not allow that which is harmful to your spirit. Prepare for war and dress for the battle; the hour to advance has come. Be watchful and keep a ready ear to receive your instructions and plan of attack. We continue to move forward in the spirit of the Lord and the power of his might. **#TeamNoFear**

Day 120
TODAY'S WORD! Accepting the will of God for your life may not be as easy as you think. At times you may doubt because the path gets extremely difficult. You may also want to believe that there is another route to the same destination. Jesus prayed three times while accepting the will of the father. Ultimately, your decision must be "NOT MY WILL,

BUT YOURS BE DONE" no matter the present circumstances. Your faith must be unwavering, and your heart must be committed to the will of God. You must know that his plan for you is good and never allow doubt and unbelief to find its way in your life. This life is temporary, so never invest all that you have in something temporary. However, we have a life that is eternal, and that life is everlasting with God the Father. Not my will, but yours be done! **#TeamNoFear**

Day 121

TODAY'S WORD! Don't waste your time and energy on useless nonsense. For one day, you will look up and ask yourself where has all my time gone? Be watchful of "time bandits and dream killers," for they seek out the less committed. Faith comes by hearing the word, and results come by acting on it. Therefore, make all your actions without hesitation. Be careful not to give time to those who look to keep you sidetracked. Continue to focus on the task at hand. There is much work to be done, and you have your assignment, so go forth. Search for truth and let the lies of your enemies be lost like a ship at sea. Remain focus and committed to God's purpose for your life and watch the blessings flow as waves upon the shore. Continue to move forward in the Lord and the power of his might. **#TeamNoFear**

Day 122

TODAY'S WORD! Greater things are coming so continue to move forward and faint not. As a Christian, our life begins when this one ends; therefore, never trouble yourself over that which is temporary. Look to the eternal kingdom of God, which is everlasting. Jesus went to the cross, then to the tomb, and three days later, he rose with all power to do something greater. Find joy in the fact that our Savior is alive and still making way for us. So why fear the things of this life when you know that they are only temporary? Why fear death when you know that life begins after it? Why fear hardships and dark times when the (Son) has already given us the victory? All power belongs to God; therefore, walk in the spirit of the Lord and the power of his might. **#TeamNoFear**

Day 123

TODAY'S WORD! In the middle of it all, be of good courage, and he shall strengthen your heart all ye that hope in the Lord. Life was never supposed to be easy. If it was, how could we ever expect to grow? Some lessons are hard, and others are harder, but through it, all God will forever make away. In the middle of your hardships, walk with your head held high for GREATER IS HE THAT IS IN YOU, THEN HE THAT IS IN THE WORLD. Know that you can do all things through Christ who strengthens you. So, say to your big problems that my God is bigger and say to your situation you are only temporary, but my God is eternal. The words you allow to exit your mouth are vital to your survival, so speak words that bring life and not death. Speak words that bring victory and not defeat, so that you may keep the upper hand on your adversary. **#TeamNoFear**

Day 124

TODAY'S WORD! If your vehicle ran out of gas, would you fill your gas tank up with kerosene? NO, because your vehicle would not function properly, and it will cause extensive damage. Would you make Kool-Aid with salt? NO, because it would taste awful, and the sweetness that you savor to would be lost. So, why on earth would you allow those things that are not of God into your spirit? You must be very careful with what you allow for entertaining you and asking yourself how it is helping you. Our enemy is very strategic in his planning and is only focuses on your failure. It is small and the "harmless things" that cause the most damage. Listen to what is not said and look for what is not often seen, so that you may always stay ready. Set yourself up for success by helping your enemies less! **#TeamNoFear**

Day 125

TODAY'S WORD! You WILL have hardships, downfalls, and disappointments in this life; God's Word will ALWAYS remain the same. You may feel alone and depressed, frustrated, and like all hope is lost, but the word of God remains the same. He is the same yesterday, today, and forever. Heaven and earth will pass away before his Word fails. Therefore, stand on that which is forever. Hold tight to that which is eternal and everlasting because they will bring life where there is death and hope where there is hopelessness. Stand in agreement with that which can bring peace where there are chaos and love where there is hate. Allow the word of God to find a place to dwell in your heart so that when you face difficult situations in this life, victory will be yours in every area. May these words encourage you today and reach you in your time of need. May the God of our salvation continue to move you forward. **#TeamNoFear**

Day 126

TODAY'S WORD! There will come a time in your life when your financial status, job title, fame, and fortune will mean absolutely nothing. Your education, looks, and the number of people you know will be worthless. This time in your life will be when you get introduced to the reality of the real world. You can name drop and flash a bunch of cash, but it will do no good. You can submit your application based on your qualifications and the many degrees you hold but still be denied. It isn't until you humble yourself under the mighty hand of God and rid yourself of self-praise that you will truly experience the awesome power of God. #TeamNoFear

Day 127

TODAY'S WORD! To accept the fact that God's will is best for me is not always the easiest thing to do. When you come to a point in your life when you can say, "NOT MY WILL BUT YOUR WILL BE DONE, it opens up so many areas in your walk with him. Knowing that his plan and his purpose is best will keep your feet firmly on the ground and will continue to give you the strength to move forward. You should fully trust his plan and to stand in faith in his Word, which will bring you through any situation. I am a living witness of his awesome working power after submitting and committing to his will, which is where your strength resides. Against all the odds, stand in faith, the face of your worse fears, you will find victory and peace in the middle of your storm. Leaning not to my own understanding but acknowledging Him in all my ways has brought me through. **#TeamNoFear**

Day 128

TODAY'S WORD! As I reflect on the past couple of days, I am reminded that in my weakness, Christ is my strength. I am reminded that in my sorrow, Christ is my joy. To be in a position were all my strength and knowledge means absolutely nothing; I now understand what it truly means to TRUST IN THE LORD! **#TeamNoFear**

Day 129

TODAY'S WORD! Why worry about those things you cannot change? Do what you can and allow God to work his plan. You cannot be everywhere, doing everything, so allow God to work his plan. Do not sit back but focus on the task at hand. Seek first the kingdom of God and his righteousness and all things will be added unto you. Your faith and action on your part are the key ingredients to a successful life. Faith without works is the ingredients for failure; therefore, waste not your time on foolishness and nonsense. There is work to be done, and you have been called for such a time as this. **#TeamNoFear**

Day 130

TODAY'S WORD! There is a plan for your life and directions on how to get to your destination. By choosing not to spend time in the Word and prayer, you will never find out. The plan may not be fully revealed, and you may not make it to your destination. The children of Israel wandered for 40 years because of their lack of faith and selfishness. You must fully commit and submit to the will of God and walk in faith despite adversity. You must continue to move forward through the storms and press on through the hardships to obtain what is yours. Giving up is not an option if you want to attain greatness. **#TeamNoFear**

Day 131

TODAY'S WORD! In this life, you cannot avoid hardships; they come only to make you strong, so why complain. It is in your best interest to look for opportunities to get stronger, physically, and spiritually. A warrior trains for battle, but a coward runs and hides. A coward complains about training and the journey he or she must face. Also, at times they complain about the enemy and the force that is used against them. So, today drop your cowardly fleshly armor and put on the armor of God. **#TeamNoFear**

Day 132

TODAY'S WORD! Though our outward man perishes daily, our inward man is renewed day by day. Therefore, look to build that which is eternal and let that which is temporary fall by the wayside. Your work is significant, and the time you have been given is short, so focus on the task at hand. Speak words of life and do your work with helping hands, so that you may receive your blessings. Be sure to build up and not tear down. Plant the seeds you have been given because one day, it will rain. May the Lord of our salvation continue to move us forward. **#TeamNoFear**

Day 133

TODAY'S WORD! There is a focus and a commitment required to move forward in the things of God. There are sacrifices and a determination required to move forward in the things of God. There is forgiveness and humbleness required to move forward in the things of God. Those who are willing to submit and commit to God's plan completely will move forward, and those who are not will continue to go over the same lesson. There will be no force involved with your decision making; it must be because you want to. Your faith and your actions are vital to your success. **#TeamNoFear**

Day 134

TODAY'S WORD! The good news is that you woke up this morning, fully equipped with the tools you need to be a blessing to someone. Start your day by giving praise to God and ask him to lead you to those who need to hear this good news. **#TeamNoFear**

Day 135

TODAY'S WORD! Making decisions based on the Word of God and not on how you feel is not always the easiest thing to do. You must learn to walk in the spirit and faith. Take God's Word at face value and step out on faith, believing that he is able. Allow him to show you his mighty hand and his marvelous works. Give no room to doubt and unbelief, for they both will come to uproot the seed that has been planted. Guard your heart and pray for discernment so that you won't be deceived. May the Lord of our salvation continue to move us forward. #TeamNoFear

Day 136

TODAY'S WORD! Each day you live, you are given another chance to do better than you did yesterday. Continue to press forward, trusting that God will see you through every hardship. It is his hand that gets the work done; you are just a vessel, so allow his plan to work in your life. You need to commit and submit so that you will be made whole and nothing, but greatness will shine through. His righteousness is perfect, and His Word is true, so stand in faith and move in action. For today is your day for victory and change. **#TeamNoFear**

Day 137
TODAY'S WORD! Lean not to your understanding, but acknowledge God in all your ways, and he will direct your path. Begin to see things the way God sees them. Begin to speak His Word over your life in every area, but to do that, you must first remove your eyes off the flesh and renew your doubtful mindset. You must starve those things that are contrary to the Word of God and uproot everything that does not produce love. With every action, act in faith and move forward in confidence, knowing that greater is he that is in you than he that is in the world. **#TeamNoFear**

Day 138
TODAY'S WORD! Walk in the spirit and in love, sowing seeds that will bear good fruit every chance you get. Look to lend a helping hand whenever possible and give no room to hatred. Guard your

heart and protect the ground where your seeds are sown, for it is vital to your survival. Allow God to do his work even if it is uncomfortable to your flesh, and the results will be perfect. Feed your spirit man daily, for our enemy is not flesh and blood. Continue to move forward and grow or sit still and perish, and you have been given a choice since the beginning of time. **#TeamNoFear**

Day 139
TODAY'S WORD! Don't think for one minute you are saved by your good deeds or by the works of your hands. Don't think that your righteousness is what gets you in good graces with God. Don't think that because you don't smoke or drink, that you have more favor then your fellow brother. The fact is God shows mercy to whom He pleases, and Jesus came for all who would receive him. Salvation is available to all, but you must receive it and act on the word of God accordingly. **#TeamNoFear**

Day 140
TODAY'S WORD! The Word of the Lord comes

to bring you strength and to encourage you in your time of need. It brings love and salvation, hope, and peace. However, you must receive it into your heart and act on it by faith to see results. The Word of God is like dynamite, mighty when the fuse is lit. If the fuse is never lit, you never experience the life-changing power. So today, set fire to the fuse and be ready for change. **#TeamNoFear**

Day 141
TODAY'S WORD! There will always be hardships and disappointments in this life. Remember always to keep these things in mind, trouble don't last always, and greater is coming. Why worry about something temporary? Why stress about things you cannot change? The sun will rise; rather, you want it to or not. The rain will fall when you have plans to be outside, and there will be nothing you can do about it. So, enjoy the sun and dance in the rain every chance you get. **#TeamNoFear**

Day 142
TODAY'S WORD! No matter what you may be

going through, you can choose to be encouraged. You can complain about the rain, or you can choose to dance in it. You can cry about having lemons or make lemonade; nothing will get better until you make a choice to do better. Stop allowing the enemy to use your mouth to speak. Instead, speak the Word of God over your life and walk in faith; after all, the choice is yours. **#TeamNoFear**

Day 143
TODAY'S WORD! Look to God for your award and promotion or whatever it is that you think is good for you. If you depend on man, you will be disappointed and upset, not to mention setting yourself up for failure. Man cannot set a permanent blessing in place, nor can he open a door God has shut. The power of man is a smokescreen, and in all his strength is false hope. If you want to be sure of victory, then put your complete trust in the Lord, and he will direct your path. **#TeamNoFear**

Day 144
TODAY'S WORD! This is the day that the Lord has

made; therefore, be a blessing to someone. Look for an opportunity to speak life to someone dead. Look to encourage those who are discouraged and share the love with those who feel unloved. Allow the spirit of God to guide you and give you the strength to move forward. Keep in mind that greater is he that is in you, than he that is in the world. Know that you can do all things through Christ, who strengthens you and at all times guard your heart, for our enemy is always looking for an opportunity to kill, steal, and destroy. May the Lord of our salvation continue to move us forward, fearlessly in faith. **#TeamNoFear**

Day 145

TODAY'S WORD! Put those things which are heavy in the hands of the Lord, so that you may continue to walk the path. Never allow negative words to impact your life, for they are like arrows aimed at your heart. Flee from people who speak doubt and unbelief so that those seeds will not be planted in your life. God is working the plan for your life, so focus on what is important and give no time to foolishness and nonsense. Do not spend any time in the company of those who give false witnesses, for they just may turn on you. **#TeamNoFear**

Day 146

TODAY'S WORD! You cannot continue to speak words of doubt and unbelief with the hope of moving forward. You cannot continue to worry about what other people may say or think about you with the hope of moving forward. Speak the Word of God over your life and move forward in faith, standing on God's Word. Looking at a hurdle and never jumping, it will turn that hurdle into a roadblock. There are a plan and purpose for your life; choosing to waste your time and energy on foolishness and nonsense is not wise. Focus on the task at hand and let that which is not a good fall to the wayside. **#TeamNoFear**

Day 147

TODAY'S WORD! You are wonderfully and beautifully made, handcrafted by God himself. You are his most priceless creation, and he cares for you beyond measure. Know that he watches over you like a hawk and protects you against all harm. He makes your paths straight and your burden easy to bear. He hears your voice late in the midnight hour and early morning. His love for you is immeasurable, and hope for change has been placed on the inside of you. Therefore, yield to the leading of his spirit and receive your instructions for a dynamic change today. #TeamNoFear

Day 148

TODAY'S WORD! Be transformed by the renewing of your mind and begin to allow God's Words to become your words. Walk in the spirit and in love to find that there is no enemy too powerful. Waste, not the little time you have on foolishness and nonsense, because there is work to be done. If you cannot agree with someone, walk away on peaceful terms, and allow the day to continue. Stop complaining and start doing, and you will find change over the horizon. Expect great things to happen when you choose to move forward. #TeamNoFear

Day 149

TODAY'S WORD! Accepting who you are with all

your flaws and faults is the first step in the right direction. God already knows all of you, so trying to hide it will do nothing but prolong your progress forward. Continue to press forward, trusting that God has given you the victory in every area. Walking in the spirit and standing in faith are the keys to success. Be watchful with every step for the enemy looks for any opportunity to keep you at a standstill. Know that with no forward motion, you will always remain in the same place, so today, GET MOVING! #TeamNoFear

Day 150

TODAY'S WORD! The more you complain, the less you will get done, so work more and complain less. What do you expect to receive with no effort on your part? How can you expect better with no change in your lifestyle? If you continue to pay attention to others, making that your daily work, you will cause yourself to fall short. Doing the same thing day in and day out will yield the same results. If you want to change, work it, speak it, do it until it happens. Nothing from nothing leaves nothing. #TeamNoFear

Day 151

TODAY'S WORD! Be persistent and consistent in your everyday actions, which draw you closer to God. Be mindful of the words that exit your mouth, for life and death is in the power of the tongue. Give no time and energy to foolishness and nonsense, for there are many people assigned to keep you sidetracked. Remain focused on the task at hand and never engage in unproductive conversations. No man or woman holds your destiny, nor can they stop your blessings. So today, focus on what God has called you to do and speak what God has spoken. #TeamNoFear

Day 152

TODAY'S WORD! There are opportunities in front of you every day, but only if your eyes are open and you are focused. Preparing yourself before you leave your home is vital to your success. Spend time with the Lord in meditation and worship. You will receive your instructions and be able to move forward towards your destiny and purpose. You will be able to see the set up before you are set up for our

135

adversary. You will be able to hear what is not spoken so that you can plan accordingly. You will be able to see the signs, so that you may stay the course. Only if you are prepared and ready beforehand, so take the time to get ready so that you can be ready. **#TeamNoFear**

Day 153
TODAY'S WORD! This is the day that the Lord has made, so rejoice and be glad in it. Be glad that you have been allowed to see how beautiful it is. Be glad that you can be a blessing and lend a helping hand. Be glad that you have been delivered and set free. The Lord is great and mighty, and his hand is strong. Move forward in confidence and faith; for this day, the Lord has given you everything. **#TeamNoFear**

Day 154
TODAY'S WORD! Remain focused on the task at hand, for the time you have been given is not long. Guard your heart against those who may speak words of doubt and unbelief, for these are the seeds of failure. Continue to move forward in faith for God

has already given you the victory. Let not your failures and setbacks cause you to give up, for they are the very reason you get stronger. So today, allow God to help you with your calling and keep your mouth shut and listen to his instructions. **#TeamNoFear**

Day 155
TODAY'S WORD! With each day that passes, look to better yourself and follow the path that leads to improvement. No one is self-made, but it is by the hand of God that they were crafted. So, look towards him for guidance and directions, for he knows all and sees all. Submit and commit to God's will, and there will be victory over every enemy for the Lord our God is mighty in battle. Lift your hands and rejoice for gladness will fill our hearts, and praise will be on our lips. Today is beautiful, and I am wonderfully made in the image of God. **#TeamNoFear**

Day 156
TODAY'S WORD! The Lord, our God, is great and mighty; he can heal and set us free. Let us give him praise and lift his holy name both now and forever.

Let us worship him in spirit and truth, giving him glory beyond measure. Let us submit to his will and commit to his plan so that we may fulfill our calling. Let us remain

humble so that he may be exalted high above the earth. Let us forever keep his word in our hearts and his praises on our lips. Mighty and holy is the Lord of host, God, our Savior. **#TeamNoFear**

Day 157

TODAY'S WORD! God has created you for something great. He had a plan in mind when he made you. There is a purpose for your life, and he has called you to do a job. However, our adversaries want the opposite of that and will do anything to void what God has for you. Therefore, stay the course and remain focused on that which is of God. Listen, learn, and receive your daily instructions so that you may obtain victory. **#TeamNoFear**

Day 158

TODAY'S WORD! Expect great things to happen, for you are a child of the King and nothing but the best is in store for you. Why complain about those things which are temporary and subject to change at any given moment? Instead, rejoice in that which is eternal and everlasting for these things will never end. No enemy will find victory, and no set back will be a failure, for all things will work in your favor. So, today stand and move forward, for this is the day that the Lord has made. **#TeamNoFear**

Day 159

TODAY'S WORD! Take each day as it comes and trusts that the Lord will supply your every need. Lean not to your understanding, but acknowledge God in all your ways, and he will direct your path. It is guaranteed that with each day you face, there will be a hill to climb, but if you refuse to give up, victory will be yours. Be honest with yourself and allow God to help you in every aspect of your life. Keep the words you speak in line with the Word of God and stand in faith. **#TeamNoFear**

Day 160

TODAY'S WORD! There is power in the name of

Jesus, so stand in confidence when you face hardships. Walk-in faith when you face opposition, knowing that victory and deliverance are yours. Shout from the mountain tops that our Savior lives, and all power has been given to him. Death, hell, nor the grave couldn't hold him. Therefore, rejoice and be glad for our life is everlasting. So, fear not in this life, for it will pass like a vapor and soon be gone like the seasons. #TeamNoFear

Day 161

TODAY'S WORD! Choosing to not move forward because of fear will eventually leave you defeated. God has not given us a spirit of fear. Therefore, never hesitate to move forward in confidence and faith. Victory only goes to those who are willing to step out on faith. You will never get anything accomplished, walking hand and hand with fear. You will never score a point if you are afraid to take a shot. You will never reap a harvest if you are afraid to get dirty. So today, break up with fear and allow yourself to experience a whole new life, not being afraid. #TeamNoFear

Day 162

TODAY'S WORD! Be encouraged for the Lord; our God is mighty in battle. There is no victory if there is no faith, and there is no faith if there is no action. You have been given the option, and the choice is yours to act or not to act. You can choose to stand still or move forward towards victory and a better way of life. **#TeamNoFear**

Day 163

TODAY'S WORD! You can choose to give up, or you can choose not to. You can choose to stand still, or you can choose to move forward. You can choose to accept what the Word of God says about you or choose not to accept it. The point is that the choice is yours; therefore, make decisions that will better you and those around you. Today think before you act and listen before you speak, or you may risk missing something essential. **#TeamNoFear**

Day 164

TODAY'S WORD! You should look forward to changing, for, without change, things will forever remain the same. Seasons change, and people change; however, God remains the same, and his word never fails. Therefore, stand in faith and walk in confidence, knowing that our God is God. Move forward, knowing that all power has been given to him, and there is no enemy too great. God causes change to happen, but you must accept it; therefore, you should look forward to it and expect great things to happen. #TeamNoFear

Day 165

TODAY'S WORD! Be grateful for the things you have, such as health and strength, for man did not provide these. Lift your hands and rejoice, for man cannot charge you a fee to keep them. Be thankful that God continues to allow you to have them. Today sing with your mouth, clap with your hands, and dance with your feet, for God has given you great gifts. #TeamNoFear

Day 166

TODAY'S WORD! Why compare your life to someone else's? What good will it do? They were created for a purpose, and so were you, so that should be your focus. No one was made like you. God created you perfectly, and he has a plan for your life. Seek, and you will find. Knock, and the door will open. Ask, and you shall receive. A big house, a fast car, and fancy clothes are not the fruits of success. However, improving someone's life physically and spiritually cannot be taken away. So, seek your purpose, receive your instructions, and be successful today. **#TeamNoFear**

Day 167
TODAY'S WORD! The words you allow to exit your mouth will have an impact on your surroundings. The way you carry yourself and the company you keep will have an impact on your life. Let your words agree with the Lord, allowing the spirit of God to accompany you. **#TeamNoFear**

Day 168
TODAY'S WORD! God is working on your behalf and always has your best interest in mind. Therefore, do your part by standing on his word and walking in

faith, knowing that victory is yours. Guard your heart and be mindful of your tongue, not giving any room to the adversary. Today stand and walk in faith, knowing that God's Word will never fail. **#TeamNoFear**

Day 169

TODAY'S WORD! This is the day that the Lord has made; he has given it to you as a gift. Therefore, lift your hands and rejoice for the Lord our God is great. Even though the storms may come, they will pass, and the sun will shine again. Even though we go through trials and tribulations, at the end of them all, we will be victorious. Know that all things will work in our favor, so move forward in faith and confidence. The Lord, our God, is mighty and strong in battle. **#TeamNoFear**

Day 170

TODAY'S WORD! As you go about your day, look for God in conversations with people. Look for him in the actions of others; he is right by your side and just maybe trying to tell you something. In all that you do and say, keep God a part of it. For he is your help and your protection in every situation you face daily. **#TeamNoFear**

Day 171

TODAY'S WORD! Trusting in the Lord, no matter where you are in your life will cause your faith to grow. Hearing the Word of God and applying it to your life will cause your faith to grow. Stepping out on faith will cause you to trust God more and more each day. However, standing still and refusing to move forward because fear will cause you to remain where you are. Today trust the Lord and step out on faith and watch the wonderful things he does. **#TeamNoFear**

Day 172

TODAY'S WORD! Faith without works is dead, so how can you expect God to move when you choose to stand still? How can you expect change when you choose to continue to do the same things? How do you expect victory when fear is your friend? God will not move until you move in faith, and nothing will change until you do something different. There will not be a victory until you unfriend fear. **#TeamNoFear**

Day 173
TODAY'S WORD! If God has allowed you to see another day, try to make a difference in someone's life. Give no more time to foolishness and nonsense and lend a helping hand whenever possible. Share the good news that Jesus Christ is alive and has come to save lives. Lift your hands in worship and rejoice in the fact that this life is only temporary and greater is in store. Sing a song of praise for our God is God, and there is none above him. **#TeamNoFear**

Day 174
TODAY'S WORD! May the word of the Lord bring joy to those who receive it, and may his spirit forever walk with those who believe. The Lord, our God, is mighty and strong in battle; therefore, let us rejoice, singing mighty is our God. He gives us strength in time of need and healing in a time of sickness; mighty and merciful is the Lord our God. **#TeamNoFear**

Day 175
TODAY'S WORD! What would cause you to doubt God? What could cause you not to trust the Lord? How dark would it have to be for you to be afraid? If you ever find yourself in any situation where these questions cross your mind, just take a deep breath, and realize that he is keeping you alive at that very moment. Just look outside and look at his awesome work. Just listen to the sounds with the ears he has given you. Just move your arms and legs or open your mouth and begin to thank him and watch how fast things change. **#TeamNoFear**

Day 176
TODAY'S WORD! Let not your heart be trouble for this life will pass away along with the problems that are in it. Soon there will be nothing but joy and peace everlasting. You will no longer have pain and sorrow, and no more hate and evil acts of men. There will no longer be efforts to pile currency as high as the sky and carrying the stress of debt will be no more. Rejoice! There is a place for those who have accepted Jesus Christ as their personal Lord and Savior.

#TeamNoFear

Day 177
TODAY'S WORD! Sing praises unto the Lord our God, for he is great. Let not your heart be troubled by that which is temporary and will soon pass away like the seasons. Let not your enemies steal your joy, for they seek to hinder your progress. May your ears be unplugged, your eyes open, and your heart receptive to the Word of God always. **#TeamNoFear**

Day 178
TODAY'S WORD! There are decisions you must make every day in life; when doing so, be sure you can deal with the consequences of those decisions. Never make your decisions based on what other people may think. Remember, this is your life that you must live it. There were many things Jesus did that people didn't like; however, he had to do his father's will. You will never make everyone happy all the time. The sun will shine when people want it to rain, and the rain will fall when people want the sun to shine. Stand firm during your storm and continue

148

to move forward. **#TeamNoFear**

Day 179

TODAY'S WORD! Keep moving forward, walking in faith, and standing on God's Word. There will be bumps in the road but maintain your balance and keep pushing. There will be potholes, but know that with each one you face, your strength will increase. There may be speed bumps but taking your time and getting your instructions will ensure your victory. Under all circumstances, trust God and lean not to your understanding, for he will make your road smooth again. **#TeamNoFear**

Day 180

TODAY'S WORD! You can believe in God all day long, but it will not get you results, and his hand will not move. It takes faith to please God, and faith is an action word. You must begin to operate in faith and apply the word of God in your life to see change. You get out what you put in. If you put in drama and negativity, how can you then expect good? You will not grow a Peachtree by planting apple seeds; Therefore, examine your mouth and make changes accordingly. Today is the time to uproot the weeds in your life, for you to see the flowers. **#TeamNoFear**

Reflections/Notes:

Reflections/Notes:

Reflections/Notes:

153

Reflections/Notes:

Reflections/Notes:

Day 181

TODAY'S WORD! This is the day that the Lord has made, so rejoice and be glad in it. Why do you complain when God has shown you enough grace to wake you up in your right mind? Why do you complain when he has given you the use of all your limbs? Open your eyes and put important things into perspective. Be grateful for God has given you gifts that man could never give. So today, lift your hands and rejoice for God has shown you grace and mercy once again. #TeamNoFear

Day 182

TODAY'S WORD! Your faith, along with your actions, moves the hand of God. Your success is molded by your words, the renewing of your mind, and your actions. People only play a small part in making this happen, so don't think for one minute that someone else holds the key to your success. Look towards the Lord for guidance and directions, for he knows the way. Lift your hands and surrender every area of your life for change and healing. Today is a new step in the right direction for awesome is the

Lord our God. **#TeamNoFear**

Day 183

TODAY'S WORD! May the Lord of our salvation continue to move you forward, and may he continue to fill you with joy. May he continue to shield you from all hurt, harm, and danger while providing you with safety, wherever you may go. May he bring you the desires of your heart as you serve him every day, humbling yourself under his mighty hand. Continue to submit and commit to his will, so that your instructions may be clear. **#TeamNoFear**

Day 184

TODAY'S WORD! Be thankful for what you have been given. These are things which man can't take away. Live each day as if it was your last, and let love find you wherever you are. Lift your hands because you can and sing songs of praise unto the Lord. Embrace each day and look forward to the things that come with it. With each step you take, it brings you closer to your destination; therefore, continue to move forward. **#TeamNoFear**

Day 185

TODAY'S WORD! You must choose victory, or you will be met with defeat. You must choose to keep moving forward, or you will sit still and accomplish nothing. You must choose not to give up, or you will fail in every effort you put forth. The power of choice has been given to you by God himself, so use it to obtain victory and success today.
#TeamNoFear

Day 186

TODAY'S WORD! Stay the course for victory is yours, said the Lord. Let not your heart be troubled by the opposition, for it comes to make you strong. Let not the words of your enemies make room in your heart where the Word of the Lord should reside. Be filled with joy, for it is the strength of the Lord in your time of need. Speak that which God has spoken, so that you may obtain victory over every enemy.
#TeamNoFear

Day 187

TODAY'S WORD! Investing time and energy into

something out of your control is placing your seeds on a concrete sidewalk. This foolish act will not bring you a harvest, nor will it release the full potential of your seed. Your valuable seed will only wither away, dry up, and die. To get the maximum results, plant your seeds in fertile ground, which will result in maximum growth. Allow the word of God to increase your faith and act on it to move you forward. #TeamNoFear

Day 188

TODAY'S WORD! Faint not, for victory is yours, said the Lord. I will cause your enemies to become confused. I will open many doors that seem to be locked and cause blessings to flow like the rivers. I will make your path straight and give you instructions to overcome. Humble yourself and submit to my will and watch my mighty hand move in your favor. #TeamNoFear

Day 189

TODAY'S WORD! Today is a new beginning, a chance to start over, and an opportunity to make better decisions. Look at your inner circle and the actions of those in it and make your changes accordingly. People either add, multiply, or subtract from your life, so pay very close attention to what they are doing. Never allow too much subtracting, because eventually, you will end up with nothing. Pray for wisdom and guidance so that the Lord may lead you towards your destiny and purpose. #TeamNoFear

Day 190

TODAY'S WORD! Never give people the power to validate who you are. Never allow people's perception of you to dictate your day. Never allow people's negative comments to have power over the way you feel. God created you perfect, and there is no such thing as a mistake in his work. So today, walk with your head held high and in faith, knowing that God created someone GREAT. #TeamNoFear

Day 191

TODAY'S WORD! Open your eyes and lift your hands, for once again, the Lord has made a way. Sing songs of praise and thanksgiving for the Lord has once again provided. The Lord, our God, is great and full of mercy and grace. How wonderful it is to serve a mighty God, which no enemy can stand in victory. All the heavens and earth will forever worship and say mighty is our God. **#TeamNoFear**

Day 192
TODAY'S WORD! May the Lord of our salvation continue to move you forward, so that your purpose may be fulfilled. May he fill you with his joy, every day, for the joy of the Lord is our strength. May he continue to watch over you so that the enemy may find no way to confuse. May he bring you peace in your time of need, so that you may find comfort in trying times. Mighty and awesome is our God whose kingdom will reign forever and ever. **#TeamNoFear**

Day 193
TODAY'S WORD! Live today as if it was your last day and let not fear finding any room in your home. Walk in the spirit and stand in faith, so on that today, you may find confidence in the Lord. Abide in love

and walk hand and hand with forgiveness, so that your heart won't be hardened. May your ears be unplugged that you may hear, and your eyes opened, so that you may see. May your heart be receptive to the Word of the Lord that you may receive. Today is your day **#TeamNoFear**

Day 194
TODAY'S WORD! Thank you, Lord, for watching over me and protected me every day. Thank you for your grace and mercy with every step I take. Without you, I am nothing. I am lifeless and doomed from the start. But in you, I live, move, and everything is good and working in my favor. It is because of you that I am, and I say thank you. **#TeamNoFear**

Day 195
TODAY'S WORD! How you look at your situation can make all the difference in the world. Refusing to give in to negative pressure and accepting the Word of God is the key to victory. Never allow something temporary to impact you for eternity. This life will soon pass away, and greater is coming. What good

162

will it do you to make plans to stay here, when that is not God's plan. **#TeamNoFear**

Day 196
TODAY'S WORD! Give no room to the enemy, for he looks to kill, steal, and destroy all that is good. Let the words you speak be those of love and peace so that there will be no confusion among your brothers and sisters. Walk in the spirit, so that you may receive your instructions to obtain victory. Do not be discouraged by trials and hardships, for they come to make you stronger. **#TeamNoFear**

Day 197
TODAY'S WORD! Even though things may seem hard right now, know that our God is God, and there is none above him. Know that greater is coming and that you have your blessings right now. Know that he has already made a way and that he has already provided your every need. Know that he will never leave you nor forsake you. He forever has your best interest in mind. Therefore, rejoice and lift your hands in victory and worship the Lord our God

today. **#TeamNoFear**

Day 198

TODAY'S WORD! Fear not for victory is yours, said the Lord. If you chose to walk in faith and believe my Word, I would bring down the walls that have blocked your blessings. I will cause your seeds to multiply and bring them to full bloom. I will move the stumbling blocks and cause them to become steppingstones for you. I will cause your enemies to become confused and scattered, so that you may advance. I will bring light to you in your most darkness hour and cause you to see over the mountains. Trust in me and stand on my word and you will be a witness to my mighty works, said the Lord of host. **#TeamNoFear**

Day 199

TODAY'S WORD! If you fail, that doesn't mean give up; it simply means try again or try another way. With each day comes new opportunities; therefore, be ready and look for a chance to make a difference. No one person has all the answers, so learn every chance you can. Lean not to your understanding, but acknowledge God in all your ways, and he will direct your path. **#TeamNoFear**

Day 200

TODAY'S WORD! Stay focused on the task at hand and don't give in to distractions. Follow the leading of the Holy Spirit so that you may receive your instructions. Never give in to fear, doubt, and unbelief, for they will plant seeds of destruction. Guard your heart and be mindful of your tongue, for these two things are vital to your survival. Most of all, praise the Lord our God no matter where you are in this walk called life. **#TeamNoFear**

Day 201

TODAY'S WORD! Are you letting fear hold you back from pursuing what God has for you? Are you allowing what your enemies say to affect your efforts to push forward? God has not given you the spirit of fear, and that which God has spoken has no choice but to come to pass. I encourage you today to go forward in the things of God, even in the presence of fear. I also challenge you to take the Word of God at face value and act on it. No one holds you back, but you, so get out of your way. **#TeamNoFear**

Day 202

TODAY'S WORD! Be encouraged today, for God has given us the victory over every enemy, no matter what form or shape they may appear. We have been destined for great works and greatness from the very beginning. So, let not the place you are in, on your walk, discourage you from moving forward. Give thanks to God and submit to his will for his plans for you are good. Be mindful of the words you allow to exit your mouth, for they will plant seeds of destruction. Never allow that which is temporary to affect you in any manner, for greater is in store. **#TeamNoFear**

Day 203

TODAY'S WORD! You have been given this wonderful gift called life. What you choose to do with it is up to you. Speak words that will encourage and let your actions be those of empowerment. With each step, you take, let it be that of faith and in the right direction. Stand in agreement with God's Word always and let your hands forever sow seeds in faith. Move forward, never doubting that which God has spoken, so that you may obtain victory on every hand. **#TeamNoFear**

Day 204

TODAY'S WORD! Hardships come to make you strong and help you to understand God. You would never know he was a healer unless someone was sick. You would never know he was a way maker unless someone was lost. You would never know he was a deliver unless someone was bound. Where you are in your walk with God will show you who God is, but you must act out in faith in his Word to get results. Today is your day, so own it. **#TeamNoFear**

Day 205

TODAY'S WORD! The enemy comes to kill, steal, and destroy. So, knowing this, prepare to block him from coming. Stay ready and keep a watchful eye at every turn. Guard your heart and tame your tongue, so that you give no room to the adversary. Feed that which is going to benefit your success and that which is not let it starve. Rejoice today for you have been shown mercy to be able to read these words. Now let the words of the Lord find a place in your heart so that you may find strength in your time of need. #TeamNoFear

Day 206
TODAY'S WORD! God knows all and sees all, and if he has your best interest in mind, then why worry? Lean not to your understanding, but acknowledge God in all your ways, and he will direct your path. Seek the kingdom of God and his righteousness, and all things will be added unto you. Fear not, for the Lord will bring great victory with every trial we face. We are his children, and he loves us beyond measure. #TeamNoFear

Day 207
TODAY'S WORD! If you allow God's Word to take first place when it comes to your thought process, it would be a wise decision. It will put you in a position

to see your enemies before they get within striking distance, allowing you to keep the advantage. Therefore, keep a watchful eye and a ready sword so that in that very minute, you may strike with precision and accuracy. **#TeamNoFear**

Day 208
TODAY'S WORD! If you have sown seeds, then you should expect a harvest. If you have not, then why do you waste so much time waiting for nothing? There is change waiting for you, but only if you want it and are willing to be stretched. God is looking for those who will lay aside self- elevation so that his kingdom may be advanced. So today, plant seeds in faith and submit to change, so that you may move when God moves. **#TeamNoFear**

Day 209
TODAY'S WORD! Fear not for the Lord is on our side, and there will be no enemy that will see victory against us. They will find no hope and no rest when the battle begins. They will find no refuge against us when the attack starts. Fear not said the Lord. He is

always with us and will never leave us nor forsake us. **#TeamNoFear**

Day 210

TODAY'S WORD! There are decisions you must make in life that will not always make everyone happy; however, they are decisions you must make. It is impossible to please everyone all the time. Therefore, make your decision and continue to move forward. There is a work that you must do, and you have no time to waste on foolishness and nonsense. It will rain, but the sun will shine; it will snow, and the wind will blow, but these things are out of your control. So are the things people may say and do; therefore, focus on the task at hand and continue your work. **#TeamNoFear**

Day 211

TODAY'S WORD! That which is good comes from the Lord to encourage you to continue to press forward in the things of God. It brings inspiration and salvation, along with love and compassion. Give all you have to this forward motion, for, in this direction, you will experience God's greatness. To sit still in life with no forward motion will bring nothing good; therefore, MOVE FORWARD. #TeamNoFear

Day 212

TODAY'S WORD! Never give up on yourself and never allow the words from your enemies to cause you to doubt. Trusting in the Lord and standing on his Word will increase your faith. For faith comes by hearing the Word, and results come by acting on it. Therefore, hear, listen, and do for these will help you through and bring victory and success in any given situation. #TeamNoFear

Day 213

TODAY'S WORD! As you observe the day at hand, look to seek the kingdom of the Lord. Listen to hear his Word, for it will bring you perfect peace. Make every effort to walk in the spirit, for doing so will allow you to see your adversary. Acknowledge the Lord in every way, so that he will direct your path and may he will forever continue to move you forward. **#TeamNoFear**

Day 214

TODAY'S WORD! If you spend most of your time worrying about what the enemy is saying and thinking about you, then no work will get done. Don't concern yourself with those things that will not produce good fruit; eventually, they will infect the root and destroy the whole tree. Therefore, give no time to foolishness and nonsense for these two are the building blocks to all that is unproductive. **#TeamNoFear**

Day 215

TODAY'S WORD! There is no other name whereby we must be saved; it is only in the name of Jesus that salvation is given. There is no other God above him, and there is no enemy greater. For us, God is God, and mighty is his hand. I live, move, and exist only because of him. I breathe because he blew into me the breath of life, and I will forever give him the highest praise. **#TeamNoFear**

Day 216

TODAY'S WORD! Be thankful for those things that man did not give, such as health and life, and be grateful that he cannot charge you for them. Lift your hands and rejoice, for God has given wonderful gifts. The rain has come to water our seeds, and the son has risen to give an everlasting salvation to all that will receive it. Awesome is the Lord of our salvation, and mighty is his hand. **#TeamNoFear**

Day 217

TODAY'S WORD! It takes more effort to frown than to smile and smiling brings about better results. Do those things that will improve your life instead of those that don't. Look to help instead of hurting, for it will bring about better change in your environment. And most of all, walk-in love for in it you will find no enemies. **#TeamNoFear**

Day 218

TODAY'S WORD! There will be no hiding place for the enemies of the Lord and nowhere to run. They will find no slick words to speak, nor will they have enough money to bribe. The Day of Judgment will be at hand, and all will be held accountable. Receive the gift of salvation from the Lord today, so that you won't find yourself in their shoes. #TeamNoFear

Day 219

TODAY'S WORD! For where the spirit of the Lord is, there is liberty, so may you always find yourself there. Allow the Spirit to lead you and guide you, so that your journey may be a safe one. Give time to the Word and pray so that you may receive your instructions and obtain victory. Above all, let the Word of the Lord find a home in your heart so that you may walk in love with every step you take. #TeamNoFear

Day 220

TODAY'S WORD! As you embark on a new day, consider how far the Lord has brought you. Consider all of his mighty works, the grace, and His mercy that he shows us every day. Do not forget the love shared with humankind and the salvation that has been offered to all. For the Lord, our God is awesome, both now and forever. #TeamNoFear

Day 221
TODAY'S WORD! The Lord, our God, is awesome in all his ways, and there is none above him. So, lift your hands and sing unto him the highest praise and give Him all glory and honor. For he has delivered us from the hands of our enemies and has given us everlasting, eternal life. Therefore, walk in faith and rejoice today for victory is ours. #TeamNoFear

Day 222
TODAY'S WORD! Have no fear, said the Lord, for I am he who will deliver you and bring you out. There is nothing too great or out of my reach, for I am Lord of all. Cast your cares upon me, for I care for you, and my love is unmeasurable. Trust in me and walk in faith, watching the miraculous miracles I will perform on your behalf, said the Lord of Host. #TeamNoFear

Day 223

TODAY'S WORD! Sit still and listen to the voice of the Lord, for his words will bring life. Standing in his presence will bring strength and confidence, for he is mighty in all his ways. Following his instructions will give wisdom and knowledge to victory. Therefore, pursue that which is of God and let all else fall to the ground. **#TeamNoFear**

Day 224

TODAY'S WORD! Distance yourself from foolishness and nonsense for these two will bring nothing but unproductive results. Turn your back on all that is not of God, for those things only sidetrack you from your task at hand. Never befriend fear for it looks to hold you back from your density. Therefore, trust in the Lord and stand on his Word, for this is a step in the right direction. **#TeamNoFear**

Day 225

TODAY'S WORD! Why allow an enemy that is already defeated to have victory over you? How can a lamb defeat a lion, a chicken, or an eagle? The fact of the matter is you defeat yourself by the lack of effort you put forth. You defeat yourself by complaining during your training. Therefore, shut your mouth, stop whining, and start winning. #TeamNoFear

Day 226
TODAY'S WORD! For the Lord, our God is mighty and awesome in all his ways. We have hope that the world cannot take away and an unbreakable promise. We have a love that will never fail and a joy that will endure forever. Our hope, love, and joy are in Jesus. #TeamNoFear

Day 227
TODAY'S WORD! Remember, our hope is in our Lord and Savior, Jesus Christ. It is in him, and him alone that we trust. There is no victory outside of him, and there is no defeat inside of him. Therefore, trust in him and him alone to supply your every need. Our God is awesome, and there is none above him, so invest all you have in the Lord our God. #TeamNoFear

Day 228

TODAY'S WORD! Look to the Lord for guidance and direction, for he shall make your path straight. Why waste time on temporary setbacks instead of focusing on the bigger picture? They are only setups. God will always set you in a place for success or growth; however, your eyes can cause blindness to the reality of the situation. Therefore, walk by faith and not by sight and know that God is setting you up for greatness. **#TeamNoFear**

Day 229

TODAY'S WORD! Fear not, for the Lord, our God is above all, and he can deliver you from the hands of your enemies. He can see you through your darkest hour and give you the strength to continue. Therefore, rejoice now and lift holy hands unto the Lord our God, for he is worthy of all praise. **#TeamNoFear**

Day 230

TODAY'S WORD! Be thankful that the Lord has given you breath once again. Use your voice to give him praise, dance, and clap your hands in worship, for there is none like him. How is it possible to find a place he cannot go to or a situation he cannot fix? Therefore, stand firm on his Word, and may your focus forever be fixed forward on the task at hand. **#TeamNoFear**

Day 231

TODAY'S WORD! If you are not in pursuit of God's plan for your life, then what are you doing? The world that we live in is only temporary. Why focus yourself on that which will soon pass away? Why give in to those things which will soon be no more? Why complain about those things which will soon pass like the seasons? Instead, focus on that which is eternal and surrender all of yourself to the plan and will of God. **#TeamNoFear**

Day 232

TODAY'S WORD! May the Lord of our salvation continue to move you forward towards your destiny and purpose. May he grant you unspeakable joy in your weakness, and may he shield you from all harm and danger. May your ears be unplugged, your eyes opened, and your heart is receptive to receive these words. **#TeamNoFear**

Day 233
TODAY'S WORD! Continue to press forward in the things of God so that you may fulfill your destiny and purpose. Know that the Lord our God can keep you in your darkness hour so fear not when hardships come. Speak what God has spoken and walk in faith so that you may obtain victory on every hand. For there is none greater than our God, the King of Kings, and the Lord of Lords. **#TeamNoFear**

Day 234
TODAY'S WORD! Stop beating yourself up when you fall or miss the mark. You are not perfect; neither are you able to go forward through your strength. Instead, focus on the effort you put forth in pursuing the things of God. Understand that the joy of the Lord is your strength. Know that all things will work in your favor and continue to move forward in faith, standing on the Word of the Lord. **#TeamNoFear**

Day 235

TODAY'S WORD! Stay ready and keep watch for our enemy is circling the camp. Encourage your fellow brothers and sisters for his plan is to isolate and kill. Guard your heart and be mindful of your words, for life and death are within them. The days get shorter, and time waits on no man; therefore, continue the work you have been given. In that hour, our Lord and Savior may say, well done, thy good and faithful servant. #TeamNoFear

Day 236

TODAY'S WORD! There is no enemy to fear; for the Lord, our God is above all. Receive today his salvation, mercy, and grace that is available to all. Do not pass up, not another chance to obtain this wonderful gift, for the days are getting shorter. Lift your hands to worship the only true God full of mercy and love. Rest in him, for in him, there is everything you will ever need. Shout from the mountains and rejoice in the valleys, for the Lord our God lives. #TeamNoFear

181

Day 237

TODAY'S WORD! You have come too far to turn around, and too much time has passed to give up. The race is not given to the swift, but to those who chose to persevere. When you choose to press forward, victory is the result. The ultimate prize is given to those who walk instead of sit, and who press on instead of quit. To those who pray instead of complaining, victory is yours, and the promised land is in view. So, continue to honor the Lord our God and walk in faith until you take your last breath here on earth. **#TeamNoFear**

Day 238

TODAY'S WORD! What a wonderful day! Look at the marvelous works of the Lord. Listen to the sounds of that which is in the earth. Enjoy the breath, which is from the Lord, as your heart continues to beat. Worship the Lord for who he is and thank him for what he has done. Awesome and mighty is the name of the Lord our God. **#TeamNoFear**

Day 239

TODAY'S WORD! You will experience many ups and downs in this life but know that they all will work in your favor. There is nothing that you will experience in this life that is not meant to strengthen you. In all things, consider the Word of the Lord, which is eternal and will stand at the end. The flesh is weak, but the spirit is willing, so support that which is willing and stand on that which is eternal. For in all that you face, you have the victory if you chose to walk in the spirit. **#TeamNoFear**

Day 240

TODAY'S WORD! Would you water your precious garden with kerosene? Why then would you continue to flood your spirit with foolishness and nonsense? What good will it do you to allow foxes in the chicken coops or snakes in your home? Therefore, consider all things when pertaining to the growth of your spirit man. Never allow those things which are toxic to be welcomed. **#TeamNoFear**

Day 241

TODAY'S WORD! If you want to be blessed, then be a blessing. If you want to receive, then give. If you want to find, then seek, and above all, walk-in love for in love, you will find no enemy. Be mindful of your words and pay close attention to your actions. God has a plan for your life; therefore, be prepared with ready ears and a humble heart. At all times, be ready to move without hesitation, walking in faith and confidence, knowing that our God is Lord of all. **#TeamNoFear**

Day 242

TODAY'S WORD! There is no victory outside of God, and there is no hope outside of his presence. There is no healing, no peace, no joy, and no deliverance. Therefore, walk in the spirit, welcoming the presence of the Lord our God, so that you may obtain all that is good. Lift your hands and rejoice today, for, in his presence, you stand, and victory is yours on every level. **#TeamNoFear**

Day 243
TODAY'S WORD! Would you jump if you knew you would make it? Would you take the shot if you knew it was going to go in? Would you go after it if you knew you would get it? No jump is too high, no shot is too hard, and nothing is out of God's reach. Therefore, know that greater is he that is in you, then he that is in the world. God's Word tells you to JUMP SHOOT and GO, but your faith is the first step that begins the process. **#TeamNoFear**

Day 244
TODAY'S WORD! As the sun shines and the birds fly, I will continue to give you praise. As the leaves turn colors and fall from the trees, I will continue to give you praise. As the snow falls and begins to cover the ground, I will continue to give you praise. In all things and always, I will praise the Lord of my salvation, for mighty is our God. **#TeamNoFear**

Day 245
TODAY'S WORD! Mighty and awesome is our God! His mercy and grace are eternal. His compassion

and love stretch across the oceans. He shields us from all hurt, harm, and danger, seen and unseen. He watches over us, as a mother does her infant child. He puts a hedge of protection around us so that we are safe day and night. None compares to the Lord our God. #TeamNoFear

Day 246
TODAY'S WORD! The Lord, our God, is mighty in battle, and there is no one greater. Lift your hands all nations and worship the Lord, for he is worthy of all our praise. Breaking the chains of captivity and setting the captives free by his mighty hand. Offering love and salvation to a world that is lost in the darkest darkness and doomed many generations over. #TeamNoFear

Day 247
TODAY'S WORD! Let not fear to make a home in your heart, for it is like a burglar who comes to steal your precious valuables. Give no room to doubt, for it is like a weed that grows in a garden with intentions to hold back all that is good. Therefore, confess the

word of the Lord daily and stand in faith, so that in that hour, you may have victory. **#TeamNoFear**

Day 248
TODAY'S WORD! Let not your heart be troubled, instead rejoice for the Lord our God. Let your mouth sing praises unto our King, for he has delivered us from death. Let your hands clap and be lifted for mighty is the Lord of our Salvation. Rejoice today and know that no matter what you face victory, it is yours. **#TeamNoFear**

Day 249
TODAY'S WORD! We were never meant to stay here living this momentary life. So, let not the troubles of this world bend you out of shape. We have an eternal home, which is in heaven, with our heavenly Father, where there is joy everlasting. Be not discouraged but be encouraged for greater is in store for them who have received the Lord our Savior. **#TeamNoFear**

Day 250

TODAY'S WORD! We, as men and women of God, must begin to walk in faith and not allow what we see with our eyes to discourage us. We must not allow hardships and trials to cause us to become stagnant in our walk with the Lord. If we chose not to continue forward, we would never experience all that God has for us. Therefore, in all things, continue to press forward, move with confidence in faith, knowing that the Lord our God has already made provisions for us all. **#TeamNoFear**

Day 251

TODAY'S WORD! With God, your impossible becomes possible, for all power has been given unto him. Know that in death, there is life everlasting, and no matter how bad it may seem, all things are working in your favor. Where the spirit of the Lord is, there is freedom and victory against every enemy. Submit to his will, seek the Kingdom of God, for in doing so, you shall find a hope and a joy that can never be taken away. **#TeamNoFear**

Day 252

TODAY'S WORD! There is much that has been given unto you, that which is temporary will soon pass away. However, that which is eternal will remain forever and should be your focus. Why allow the passing rain to cause you so much heartache when something greater is on the horizon? Trust in the Word of the Lord, and with every action, let faith be attached. **#TeamNoFear**

Day 253

TODAY'S WORD! May the Lord of our Salvation continue to move you forward during your storm. May he grant you the patience to wait, so that you may be complete in your work. May he deal with your enemies swiftly and cause you to rise like the sun. For our God is God, and there is no other, bless his holy name forever. **#TeamNoFear**

Day 254

TODAY'S WORD! Be not afraid for the Lord, and our God will protect us with every step we take. He will be our shelter amid the storm that we may be

189

encouraged. So, lift your voice and sing great and mighty is our God, for he has given us the victory. None can bring life and hope to a dying world and extend mercy from generation to generation. #TeamNoFear

Day 255

TODAY'S WORD! Look forward to the promises of God's Word and let no the flesh cause you to get discouraged. The spirit is willing, but the flesh is weak; therefore, walk in the spirit. Let not the words of your enemies cause you to doubt, for heaven and earth will pass away before God's Word return unto him void. Let not your eyes deceive you; instead, choose to walk by faith and not by sight. Victory is yours for the taking; choose to walk in faith, standing on the Word of the Lord, amid every storm. #TeamNoFear

Day 256

TODAY'S WORD! The Lord has allowed us to see another wonderful day. Once again, he has shown much grace and mercy to each of us. What an awesome God, who is full of love and compassion. Continue to watch over us all, Lord, as we walk the earth. May we forever continue to give you all glory and honor for the rest of our days. **#TeamNoFear**

Day 257
TODAY'S WORD! The Lord, our God, is mighty in battle, and there is no one greater. Lift your hands all nations and worship the Lord our God, for he is worthy of all our praise. Breaking the chains of captivity and setting the captives free by his mighty hand. Offering Love and salvation to a world that is lost in the darkest darkness and doomed many generations over. **#TeamNoFear**

Day 258
TODAY'S WORD! Let not fear to make a home in your heart, for it is like a burglar who comes to steal your precious valuables. Give no room to doubt, for it is like a weed that grows in a garden with intentions to hold back all that is good. Therefore, confess the Word of the Lord daily and stand in faith, so that in that hour, you may have victory. **#TeamNoFear**

Day 259

TODAY'S WORD! Let not your heart be trouble, instead rejoice for the Lord our God is God. Let your mouth sing praises unto our King, for he has delivered us from sin and death. Let your hands clap and be lifted for mighty is the Lord of our Salvation. Rejoice today and know that no matter what you face, victory is yours. **#TeamNoFear**

Day 260

TODAY'S WORD! Look up! Take time today to look up to the heavens from which blessings flow. Think about how much time we spend with your heads down, feeling defeated by the cares of this world. These cares are temporary, so why not look up and allow the Son of Man to shine down upon you. **#TeamNoFear**

Day 261

TODAY'S WORD! We, as men and women of God, must begin to walk in faith and not allow what we see with our eyes to discourage us. We must not allow hardships and trials to cause us to become

192

stagnant in our walk with the Lord. If we chose not to continue forward, we would never experience all that God has for us. In every aspect of your life, no matter the circumstance, continue to press forward, moving with confidence, knowing that the Lord our God has already made provisions for us all. **#TeamNoFear**

Day 262

TODAY'S WORD! With God, your impossible becomes possible, for all power has been given unto him. Know that in death, there is life everlasting, and no matter how bad it may seem, all things are working in your favor. Where the spirit of the Lord is, there is freedom and victory against every enemy. Submit to his Will, seek the Kingdom of God, for in doing so, you shall find a hope and a joy that can never be taken away. **#TeamNoFear**

Day 263

TODAY'S WORD! There is much that has been given unto you, which is temporary and will soon pass away. However, that which is eternal will remain forever and should be your focus. Why allow the passing rain to cause you so much heartache when something greater is on the horizon? Trust in the Word of the Lord, and with every action, let faith be attached. **#TeamNoFear**

Day 264

TODAY'S WORD! May the Lord of our Salvation continue to move you forward amid your storm. May he grant you the patience to wait, so that you may be complete in your work. May he deal with your enemies swiftly and cause you to rise like the sun. For our God is God, and there is no other, bless his holy name forever. **#TeamNoFear**

Day 265

TODAY'S WORD! Be not afraid for the Lord, and our God will protect us with every step we take. He will be our shelter amid the storm that we may be encouraged. So, lift your voice and sing great and mighty is our God, for he has given us the victory. None can bring life and hope to a dying world and extend mercy from generation to generation.

#TeamNoFear

Day 266

TODAY'S WORD! Seek a closer relationship with God. Set aside time in your "busy" schedule to read his Word and find a quiet place for you to have a conversation with him. Like any good, long-lasting relationship, what you invest in it manifests in many ways. He is worth your time because YOU are worth his. **#TeamNoFear**

Day 267

TODAY'S WORD! Continue to put forth every effort to move forward towards your destiny and purpose. Give no time to foolishness and nonsense; it will only slow you down and cause chaos in most cases. **#TeamNoFear**

Day 268

TODAY'S WORD! For the Lord has allowed us to see another wonderful day. Once again, he has shown much grace and mercy to each of us. What an awesome God, who is full of love and compassion.

Continue to watch over us all, Lord, as we walk the earth. May we forever continue to give you all glory and honor for the rest of our days. **#TeamNoFear**

Reflections/Notes:

Reflections/Notes:

Reflections/Notes:

Reflections/Notes:

Day 269
TODAY'S WORD! The Lord, our God, is working all things in your favor. For he so loved the world that he gave his only son that whosoever believe in him shall be saved. Therefore, rejoice in the fact that we have a Savior that has saved us from death and sin. He has gone away to prepare a place for us and will soon return for us again. Mighty and wonderful is the Lord our God, and beautiful are the works of his hands. #TeamNoFear

Day 270
TODAY'S WORD! Allowing God's will for your life is not always the easiest thing to do. However, if you fully submit to his will and plan for your life, you will find that things always work out perfectly. The spirit is willing, but the flesh is weak, and it is the flesh that makes the submission a little difficult. Therefore, begin to starve that which is weak and allow the spirit of God in you to flourish and bring forth greatness. #TeamNoFear

Day 271
TODAY'S WORD! What good will it do you to believe in God and not walk in faith? For it is impossible to please him without faith. You must first believe that he can, and he has already provided everything you will ever need. Faith is an action that is required on your part to move the hand of God. Fear not, instead, move forward in faith standing on his Word and witness his awesome power. **#TeamNoFear**

Day 272
TODAY'S WORD! Awesome and mighty is our God, for he has brought us out of darkness into his marvelous light. He has seen fit to bless us with health and strength for great is his mercy. His love endures from generation to generation, and he watches over us day and night. So today, and forever I will sing awesome and mighty is the Lord our God. **#TeamNoFear**

Day 273
TODAY'S WORD! If you chose not to fight, your

202

enemies would always win, and you will never get stronger. God has already given us the victory; however, we must move forward and do the work. It is your choice to give up and complain about every battle you're in, but this will do you no good. So, I say give it your all every day so that you will live life with no regrets. **#TeamNoFear**

Day 274
TODAY'S WORD! Seek the Kingdom of God, for in it all things are eternal and will last forever. Let not the temporary situations of this world hold you, for your home is not here. Be mindful that greater is on the horizon and that we serve a God who is more than able. Stand in faith and confidence that victory is yours now. Rejoice today for the Lord our God has made a way for us to succeed in all that we do. **#TeamNoFear**

Day 275
TODAY'S WORD! Jesus Christ came to deliver and set free all who are lost and dead to sin. He came to bring new life and a new beginning to all who will

accept him as Lord and Savior. His sacrifice was the stamp for redemption and hope for life everlasting. Therefore, be not discouraged, nor fearful, for we have a hope that is guarantee and victory that is undeniable. **#TeamNoFear**

Day 276
TODAY'S WORD! No matter where you are in life, never let your situations get the best of you. The things you face in this life are only temporary and will soon pass like the seasons. Therefore, rejoice today for we have an everlasting hope, which is in Christ Jesus, our Lord. Let your praise take you through whatever storm you may be in and let your worship bring the fear of the Lord upon your enemies. **#TeamNoFear**

Day 277
TODAY'S WORD! Jesus Christ is the way, the truth, the life, and there is no other way. Know that our Lord and Savior is King and has delivered us from sin and death. He went away to prepare a place for us, and with him, we will again reign forever.

Therefore, rejoice in this hope and know that there is greater on the horizon. **#TeamNoFear**

Day 278
TODAY'S WORD! Let every word be those of encouragement, causing the uplifting of your fellow brothers and sisters. Let your every thought be that of love and faith, which will keep you from falling backward. Let the works of your hands do that which will help build the Kingdom of God so that fewer will be lost. Above all, always submit to the Will of God and continue to press forward. **#TeamNoFear**

Day 279
TODAY'S WORD! Let not your heart be troubled; for the Lord, our God is mighty in battle. His reach is beyond measure, and his wisdom is unmatched. His grace and mercy endure from generation to generation. All power is given to him, and because of his spirit, we live in freedom, so rejoice today and sing mighty is our God. **#TeamNoFear**

Day 280

TODAY'S WORD! Never underestimate what God can accomplish through you if you are willing to submit to his will. Try to push forward, and God himself will give you the strength that is required to complete the task. The joy of the Lord is our strength; where the spirit of the Lord is, there is liberty and freedom. Therefore, reject all that is contrary to his will and support that which is fuel to move you forward. #TeamNoFear

Day 281

TODAY'S WORD! Learning to be comfortable in the place that God has you at this moment is very vital to your success. Whether you are in the hills or going through the valleys, know that his plan for you is good. Know that all things are working in your favor. Never hesitate to give Him praise, for it is in your praise that you experience his awesomeness. #TeamNoFear

Day 282

TODAY'S WORD! The days are shorter, and there

is still work to be done; Therefore, focus on the task at hand. Let not your hands stop working, for there are many seeds that need to be sown. Let not your voice be silent, for there are many ears that need to hear the Word of the Lord. May you be given the strength to continue what the Lord our God has called you to do and say. **#TeamNoFear**

Day 283
TODAY'S WORD! Allow the Lord to complete his work in you, so that there may be an improvement in your lifestyle. Let him uproot all that may be a hindrance, so that there may be room for growth. Allow his spirit to lead and guide you so that there will be no misunderstanding. Walk-in Love and guard your heart so that you may remain focused on your task at hand. Above all, submit to his plan and will for your life, so you may complete the work he has assigned you. **#TeamNoFear**

Day 284
TODAY'S WORD! Continue your work, standing in faith and on the Word of God, for it is a crucial

task that you have been charged with. Know that the Lord our God, has already equipped us with the tools to succeed and has given us the victory over every enemy we will face. So, knowing this, I say to you never hesitate, strike quickly, and continue to move forward for the Lord has cleared our path. #TeamNoFear

Day 285
TODAY'S WORD! The Lord, our God, is awesome! His power is unmatched, and his love extends to all generations. Receive his salvation today so that on that great day, you may be forgiven and found blameless. Receive today the sacrifice of his son, for the remission of your sins so that you may be made whole. This gift is offered freely to those that will receive and repent. Therefore, waste not another second and take hold of that which is eternal. #TeamNoFear

Day 286
TODAY'S WORD! Where the spirit of the Lord is, there is liberty, so lift your hands and rejoice now.

Dance to the joy in your heart and sing a new song unto the Lord our God. For he has made us glad and delivered us from death and sin. He has once again shown us his grace and mercy with the rising of the sun. Therefore, offer praises and bow down to the one and only true living God, the Lord, our Savior. #TeamNoFear

Day 287
TODAY'S WORD! Faint not my brother and never give up my sister for the Lord our God has given us the victory. He has brought our enemies to our feet and has canceled their plans against us. He has confused their minds and led them towards destruction to never be seen again. No weapon that is formed against us will prosper, and every plan against us will fail. Therefore, rejoice today for mighty is the Lord our God whose Kingdom will last forever. #TeamNoFear

Day 288
TODAY'S WORD! Wait on the Lord, for he shall renew your strength and bring you to the top of the

mountain. He will allow you to soar high above the hardships of this life and give you victory in every situation. Healing, deliverance, and salvation are given unto you this day if only you would receive them. So, rejoice for the Lord our God is the giver of great gifts. #TeamNoFear

Day 289
TODAY'S WORD! Here we are into another day that the Lord has made, observing the works of his mighty hands. For he is mighty, awesome, able to deliver and set free those who are bound and trapped by the enemy. He can bring love and peace, where there are hate and chaos. So, today I will offer up my praise and sing mighty and awesome is the Lord our God. #TeamNoFear

Day 290
TODAY'S WORD! Let your light shine, so that those who are in darkness may find their way. Lend a helping hand to those who are in need, so that they may follow your example. Know that the Lord our God, is clearing our path to victory and has scattered

our enemies abroad. Therefore, lift holy hands and sing mighty and awesome is our God who has given us the victory on every hand. **#TeamNoFear**

Day 291
TODAY'S WORD! Let your heart sing praises unto the Lord our God and clap your hands as loud as thunder. Dance to the medley of the joy in your heart for the Lord has made us glad. Let not the temporary things of this world hinder your praise, nor let them steal your joy. Soon they will pass away, like the seasons, and then true life will begin when we abide with the Lord our God forever. **#TeamNoFear**

Day 292
TODAY'S WORD! There is only one way to salvation, and that is through our Lord and Savior Jesus Christ. He alone can deliver us from sin and death and bring new life and hope to a lost generation. The ultimate sacrifice and the blood that was shed washed us and cleansed us from all unrighteousness. We are heirs in fellowship with the King of Kings and Lord of Lords, so rejoice now and

forever. **#TeamNoFear**

Day 293

TODAY'S WORD! With each day, continue to press forward. It is when you press into the things of God, that you receive understanding. Let not the words of your enemies find room in your heart, nor allow them to hinder your progress. Instead, confess the Word of the Lord daily, and allow it to transform your life. Move forward in faith, standing on the Word of God, and be prepared for a miraculous transformation. **#TeamNoFear**

Day 294

TODAY'S WORD! Let the spirit of the Lord guide you and let his hand deliver you out of trouble. Keep your eyes fixed on that which is eternal and press forward for the victory is already yours. May the Lord of our Salvation continue to move you forward towards your destiny and purpose. May we forever continue to give him the praise that he is due forever.
#TeamNoFear

212

Day 295
TODAY'S WORD! Lift your hands and rejoice for the Lord our God has once again cleared our path to victory. He has defeated our enemies and has blinded them, leaving them lost and confused. He has provided us with everything for our journey and given unto us many great things. So, sing a new song of praise unto the Lord our God, for he is awesome in all his ways. **#TeamNoFear**

Day 296
TODAY'S WORD! Let the Lord our God lead and guide you through your valleys so that you may travel safely. Allow him to shield and protect you from all hurt, harm, and danger. The Lord, our God, is awesome and mighty in all his ways, and his mercy endures forever. Rejoice today for our God is God, and he has come to deliver us from sin and death. **#TeamNoFear**

Day 297
TODAY'S WORD! Search the Word of God, as if it was life to a dying person or the beat to a dying

heart. For in it, you will find life, not just a temporary existence. There is hope for the hopeless and comfort to those who are lost in the darkest darkness. Therefore, continue to press on that you may find that which can deliver you no matter where you are. **#TeamNoFear**

Day 298
TODAY'S WORD! Submit to the Will of God, for in it, you will find yourself and your purpose. Walk with the Lord; in doing so, you will see yourself and the reason you were created. Listen to learn, hear to grow, and continue to move forward to obtain that which is yours. May the Lord of our salvation continue to move you forward towards your destiny and purpose. **#TeamNoFear**

Day 299
TODAY'S WORD! The Lord, our God, has already equipped you with everything you need to complete your task. However, you must move forward in faith standing on his Word. Let not your enemies cause

you to doubt and fall. Turn a deaf ear to their words, for they will be of no help to you. Remain focused on that which God has charged you with, so on that day, you will not be distracted. Continue to confess his Word and move forward in faith with each step towards your destiny and purpose. **#TeamNoFear**

Day 300
TODAY'S WORD! Continue to press in and move forward despite the opposition you may be facing. Lift your hands and give our God praise, for he remains worthy forever. Sing a new song unto our God, for he is awesome and mighty with the works of his hands. We will and shall forever confess that our God is God, and none compares. **#TeamNoFear**

Day 301
TODAY'S WORD! As you open your eyes and behold another beautiful day that God has allowed us to see, let's be thankful. As we breathe and move and begin to interact with people, let's remember his grace and mercy. Let's rejoice in the fact that he continues to watch over us during our darkest hour. Let's always

find praise in our hearts, and a kind word in our mouth for the Lord our God is great. **#TeamNoFear**

Day 302
TODAY'S WORD! I will always bless the Lord, for he has delivered me from death. He has protected me from the works of my enemies and made me a way to escape. He has given me life and loved me despite my faults and many mistakes. He has caused the sun to shine upon my face and given me grace in a brand-new day. I will forever worship the Lord our God, for he is awesome in all his ways. **#TeamNoFear**

Day 303
TODAY'S WORD! No matter who or where you are in your life, God can use you. If you step out in faith and confidence, trusting in the Word of God, he will move on your behalf. Let fear find no friend and let doubt be homeless. Instead, press forward in the work of the Lord and allow him to be your strength. May you be given a new joy and power from upon high that you may be able to fulfill your task at hand. **#TeamNoFear**

216

Day 304

TODAY'S WORD! You must understand that outside of God, and there is no life, just sin and death. There is no hope, joy, or peace. You will have no direction, instructions, or protection. For your life to be filled with life, God must be at the center of it. Therefore, submit to his will and turn your life over to him so that you might live. **#TeamNoFear**

Day 305

TODAY'S WORD! Know that no weapon that is formed against you will prosper, nor will the enemy be successful in his plans. For the Lord, our God has given us victory in every situation; not even death can win over us. Therefore, rejoice today for our God is God, and all power is in his hands. I will forever sing mighty is the Lord our God, and His Kingdom will reign forever. **#TeamNoFear**

Day 306

TODAY'S WORD! The Lord, our God, shall supply our every need, for he cares for us. He will forever make a clear path and protect us from all manners of

217

harm and danger. We can find strength in him, and with our faith, we can continue to move forward towards our destiny. Our God is God, and there is no other above him for his Kingdom shall forever reign, and His Word shall forever stand. **#TeamNoFear**

Day 307
TODAY'S WORD! There is no other name above the name of Jesus, for it is in him that we obtain deliverance for sin and death. It was his sacrifice on the cross that made us able to live where there is death. It is through him and him only that we find our way through the darkness. Therefore, rejoice and worship our God that is above all and whose Kingdom is everlasting. **#TeamNoFear**

Day 308
TODAY'S WORD! The Lord, our God, is awesome, and his mercy endures from generation to generation. Let his works be seen in all the earth and let everything that has breath praise his holy name. Rejoice and lift the name of the Lord, our God for his Kingdom will endure forever. May peace is in

every situation and love in every word, and may his spirit continue to guide us along the way. #TeamNoFear

Day 309
TODAY'S WORD! There is no one greater than our God, for he is God alone. Lift your hands in praise and worship his holy name all generations. Behold the works of his hands and set your eyes upon his marvelous works. Our God is God; therefore, let everything that is outside of his will fall by the wayside. Let every tongue confess, and every knee bow to the one and only God for his Kingdom shall reign forever and ever. **#TeamNoFear**

Day 310
TODAY'S WORD! No matter where you are in your life, be encouraged; all things work in favor of a child of God. God has your best interest at heart, and he did not bring you this far to leave you. Look towards the hills from which comes your help, lifting your hands and rejoicing for victory is yours. Fear, not those that are against you, for they will receive no

help neither will they obtain victory. Continue to press forward in faith, standing on the Word of God, for it is vital to your success. **#TeamNoFear**

Day 311
TODAY'S WORD! According to your faith, let it be so! May the Lord of our salvation continue to move you forward towards your destiny and purpose. May he subdue every enemy you encounter and cause them to fall. May he make your path straight and clear so that your feet never stumble. May he unplug your ears that you may hear, open your eyes that you may see, and minister to your heart that it may be receptive and receive the word of the Lord. **#TeamNoFear**

Day 312
TODAY'S WORD! The Lord, our God, is awesome and mighty in battle. He has supplied our every need and cleared a path to victory for us. God has delivered us from sin and death so that we may live life everlasting. He has defeated our enemies in every direction, so that we may move forward towards our

destiny and purpose. Therefore, we sing awesome and mighty is the Lord our God, who reigns with all power. **#TeamNoFear**

Day 313
TODAY'S WORD! Be very mindful of your environment, for the things and people that are in it will influence you. Be aware of your enemies and their plans, for they always wish to harm . Pray that you receive knowledge and wisdom for the days ahead unknown. Look to the Lord so that you may receive your daily instructions on how to accomplish your task. May the words of the Lord find good ground in your heart to take root and bring forth one hundred-fold. **#TeamNoFear**

Day 314
TODAY'S WORD! Sometimes you just have to put your hands to the plow and get the work done. The ground must be plowed, and the seeds must be planted. When the rain comes, it will be a joyful occasion for you now that your harvest is near. Spend

time doing the work and keep the faith in what God has promised. **#TeamNoFear**

Day 315

TODAY'S WORD! Giving your time to do the work of the Lord will eliminate a lot of unnecessary time that is wasted on nothing. Many things come to sidetrack you from the task at hand, so be watchful. Know that your work is critical to the Kingdom and that there are souls at stake. Therefore, waste not the little time you have on foolishness and nonsense. **#TeamNoFear**

Day 316

TODAY'S WORD! Be encouraged today for the Lord our God is with us! He will keep us safe from our enemies. He will provide us light in our darkest hour and lead us down the path to safety. He has given us the victory, so rejoice and sing mighty is our God, who is awesome in all his ways. Continue to press forward and bear witness to the awesome works of his hands. **#TeamNoFear**

Day 317

TODAY'S WORD! Your mouth can get you in plenty of trouble; therefore, think before you speak. Don't get so overwhelmed by your circumstances that you just act out with no regard for the consequences. Spending time in the presence of the Lord before you get your day started is a great way to be better prepared. **#TeamNoFear**

Day 318

TODAY'S WORD! Be patient and wait on the Lord, for he is making way for you. Allow God to lead you and guide you along the right path. Allow him to mold you and work on your character, for greatness will be the result. Learn to sit quietly in his presence and minister to you, for there resides unmeasurable wisdom. Receive today all that the Lord has for you and continue to move forward in faith. **#TeamNoFear**

Day 319

TODAY'S WORD! How do you expect good to come from evil works? Is it possible to produce apple trees by planting orange seeds? How can you stand on the Word of God when you don't know it? How can you walk by faith when you haven't heard it? For faith comes by hearing and hearing by the Word of God. Therefore, do good in all you do and plant those seeds which are required to bring you the correct results. Spend time in the Word and pray, so that your faith may increase, and your harvest produces. **#TeamNoFear**

Day 320
TODAY'S WORD! Trust that the Lord our God, and he will lead us down the path to victory and defeat every enemy along the way. May we continue to lift his holy name and sing praises to the highest God. May we give our whole self to his will and continue to press forward towards our destiny and purpose. Forever will his Kingdom reign, and forever will his Word stand. **#TeamNoFear**

Day 321
TODAY'S WORD! During it all, we must continue to press forward to reach our destination. There are

no short cuts and no time to waste on foolishness and nonsense. We must fully commit to God and his plan for our lives while being willing to be pushed to our limits. At all times, know this in all things, our best interest is on God's heart. **#TeamNoFear**

Day 322

TODAY'S WORD! You must have faith to please God. You must believe that he is and can. Many times, in life, we fail at this when the smallest sign of trouble shows up. We lose hope when it gets too dark and faith when things get too hard. We must hold fast to the faith we confess and to the God we serve, for in due time, all that he has promised will come to pass. **#TeamNoFear**

Day 323

TODAY'S WORD! Count your blessings! Take nothing for granted because what God does for you is done out of love. When you wake up in the morning, let praise instead of complaining be the first thing out of your mouth. **#TeamNoFear**

Day 324

TODAY'S WORD! Do you know that you are wonderfully and fearfully made? God used the best of the best materials when he made you, so don't forget this when the world tries to convince you otherwise. **#TeamNoFear**

Day 325

TODAY'S WORD! God made us several promises throughout his Word. However, he never promised that we would not have trials and tribulations. Do not waste your time asking, "why me?" instead, thank God that you are being tried, because the battle is already won. **#TeamNoFear**

Day 326

TODAY'S WORD! YOU...ARE...WORTHY! Sometimes people like to try and tell you your worth, but this is impossible for them to do because they don't know you. They didn't create, breathe life into you, or die on the cross for you, but Jesus did! He is the only one that can tell you your worth, and to him, you are priceless, so never let anyone tell you differently. **#TeamNoFear**

Day 327
TODAY'S WORD! Good deeds are not a way to earn God's favor. You already have his favor, and this is God's gift to you because he loves you. What do you do when you receive a gift? Give thanks! **#TeamNoFear**

Day 328
TODAY'S WORD! Give, if though you are giving to God. When we give our all, God acknowledges that and, in turn, gives his all to us. However, when we offer, hands out, looking for a return on our investment, we are not presenting from our heart. Christ was our example of the ultimate unconditional gift when he gave his life on Calvary. **#TeamNoFear**

Day 329
TODAY'S WORD! Be careful of the company you keep isn't just wise advice, but it is also imperative to your walk as Christian. Surround yourself with people who encourage you and cheer you on when

you stumble or fall. **TeamNoFear**

Day 330
TODAY'S WORD! Joy comes in the morning! Have you ever had something on your mind which caused you to toss and turn and lose sleep? Well, before you reach for those sleeping pills, try talking to God first. I guarantee you that whatever is troubling you that night will be replaced with joy in the morning. #**TeamNoFear**

Day 331
TODAY'S WORD! Drop that cellphone. Turn off that television. Pick up God's Word and pray for eyes to see, heart to receive, and a mind to do God's will. Taking time to seek out God's wisdom, prepares you to be a vessel, which He can use to spread the gospel. #**TeamNoFear**

Day 332
TODAY'S WORD! TODAY'S WORD! Never look at where you are but focus on where you are going. If you begin to focus on where you are, you

may become distracted and wasting a lot of time. If you begin to focus on where you are, you may become discouraged, and seeds of doubt may start to take root and grow. Have a vision and a plan, as well as dreams, goals, and a strategy in place to get there. If you don't have the least of these in place, you are sitting and spinning your wheels without forwarding motion. So, start with your vision, begin to see it, then, after that, begin to speak it and to work it. Faith without works is dead, and a vision without works has no promise. Today, focus on where you're going and remember the joy is in the journey. So never give up and never give in. **#TeamNoFear**

Day 333

TODAY'S WORD! Let the joy of the Lord dwell in your heart and let his words be found on your lips. Let your hands be lifted in praise and let your voice never cease in giving him all glory. For the Lord, our God is the ruler over all the earth and everything therein. **#TeamNoFear**

Day 334

TODAY'S WORD! Trust in the Lord, our God! He has brought us out of darkness into his marvelous light. He has delivered us from the hands of our enemies and given us freedom. He has brought healing to every sickness and light to every dark corner. He has opened our eyes to the truth and given us a heart filled with love and compassion. **#TeamNoFear**

Day 335

TODAY'S WORD! As this new day begins, I acknowledge the Lord our God, for he is awesome in all his ways. Showing grace and mercy from generation to generation and sending his only son to save and deliver the world from sin. I shall lift my hands in worship and sing praises unto the only God for the rest of my days. **#TeamNoFear**

Day 336

TODAY'S WORD! You, Oh Lord, are my strength and my hope in times of trouble. You are my way to a clear path when I am lost in darkness. You are my salvation and deliver me from sin and death. It is because of you that I can and will continue to move forward. **#TeamNoFear**

Day 337
TODAY'S WORD! The Lord, our God, will make a way to our destiny; however, we must submit to his will. We must commit to his plan and purpose for our lives. We must humble ourselves and move forward with action in faith. We must never give up nor give in to that which comes to sidetrack us from the task at hand if we want victory. **#TeamNoFear**

Day 338
TODAY'S WORD! Let not the temporary situations of this world hinder your progress forward. Instead, press on and press into the things of God, for they are eternal. Seek, so that you may find, ask that it may be given and knock, so that the door may be open. Seasons are temporary; Therefore, be as effective as possible in each of them, so that you may complete the task at hand. **#TeamNoFear**

Day 339
TODAY'S WORD! The Lord, our God, has been given all power and is for us in every aspect of life. He watches over us as a mother does her child and caring for us as well. God has met every spiritual and physical need in advance. He has answered every prayer, even before we have prayed. Therefore, walk-in confidence while standing in faith, knowing that our God is Lord of all. **#TeamNoFear**

Day 340
TODAY'S WORD! Let your every action be that of faith and without hesitation. Let your every word be that of encouragement, that it may build up and not tear down. Be on guard, so that the enemy will have no place to rest. Set your course and may every step you take to move you in that direction. **#TeamNoFear**

Day 341
TODAY'S WORD! God created you for a reason, and he has placed everything inside of you to complete your work. Therefore, move forward in

confidence, walking in faith, knowing that your every need has been met. Let not temporary situations cause you to get sidetracked, nor the words of your enemies slow you down. Keep pressing forward and watch the Lord of our Salvation work many times over. #TeamNoFear

Day 342

TODAY'S WORD! Your life is but a vapor; Therefore, walk in love and act in faith within the short time you have been giving. Seasons come and soon pass away, but love will last forever, and faith will never fail. Our God is God, and he is Lord of all; Therefore, rejoice today and sing mighty is our God. #TeamNoFear

Day 343

TODAY'S WORD! Be encouraged today, for the Lord, our God is with us and will fight for us. Let not your heart be troubled with the things of this world, for they will soon pass away. Let your focus be on that which is eternal and will never pass away. Let your words be those of encouragement, causing a forward motion in the people of God. **#TeamNoFear**

Day 344
TODAY'S WORD! May the Lord continue to push you forward towards your destiny and purpose. May he push you to pass your fears and imperfections, so that you may be bold and perfect. May he move every one of your enemies to the farthest part of the earth, so that your path may be clear. May you continue to stand on his Word and walk in faith, so that all these requests may be granted. **#TeamNoFear**

Day 345
TODAY'S WORD! Stand firm in the Word of the Lord for heaven and earth shall pass away before his Word fails. Don't give in to the pressure from the things of this world, for they are only temporary. Turn a deaf ear to the words of your enemies, for they shall fall to the ground and wither away, finding nothing but death. However, we shall find everlasting life if we chose to stand in faith and on the Word of our Lord. **#TeamNoFear**

Day 346

TODAY'S WORD! If you decide to continue to press forward during the storm, there is peace on the other side. Decide that no matter what you face, your trust and faith will be in God. Decide that you will stand on his Word no matter how dark it gets. Be persistent and consistent in every action, so that procrastination and laziness will have no place to live. **#TeamNoFear**

Day 347

TODAY'S WORD! Lift your hands and give praise to the one and only true God, full of mercy and grace. Be thankful today, for he has extended forgiveness to us all and has made our way clear. He has caused our enemies to be confused and exposed their plans to harm us. He has caused the sun to shine upon us all and filled us with a joy that the world cannot take away. Join me in singing mighty is the Lord our God, and awesome is his works. **#TeamNoFear**

Day 348

TODAY'S WORD! The Word of the Lord our God

will never fail, nor will it fall short in coming to pass. Therefore, rejoice and stand in faith on his Word, for victory is ours on every hand. Know that if you faint not, you will receive what has been promised to you from the beginning of time. The Lord, our God, is mighty in battle, and awesome are the works of his hands. **#TeamNoFear**

Day 349
TODAY'S WORD! Walk-in faith knowing that the Lord our God has made our way straight and safe. He has already confused our enemies and scattered them abroad so they cannot harm us. God has already provided our every need, no matter the situation. He will bring the rain in due season to water every seed that has been planted. Therefore, I say unto you this day, walk-in faith, and stand on the Word of our Lord for it is already done. **#TeamNoFear**

Day 350
TODAY'S WORD! There is no place in life; you cannot stand if you hold fast to your faith in the Lord our God. There is no mountain too high to climb and

no valley too deep. There is no enemy too great, and no situation too difficult to fix. Therefore, rejoice today and sing Mighty is our God. **#TeamNoFear**

Day 351
TODAY'S WORD! Wake early in the morning to give our God praise, for he is worthy. Never miss an opportunity to thank him for providing you with everything you need. Listen to your instructions and be clear on what to do. With every action, act in faith, and with every word of encouragement, the battle continues. May the Lord our God continue to move us forward. **#TeamNoFear**

Day 352
TODAY'S WORD! The focus is not on your fall or mistakes. What is important is what you do after them. You must, despite all opposition, continue to press forward. You must trust that God's Will has already worked things out in your favor. The reward is in finishing the race and not at the starting of it. **#TeamNoFear**

Day 353

TODAY'S WORD! Allow God to complete his work in your life, although it may be uncomfortable sometimes. Allow the Spirit to lead and guide you so that you may always be learning . Be slow to speak, observing your surroundings; by doing so, you will hear what is not said and see what is not shown. Be humble so that God will exalt you in due time, and his work will be completed in your life. #TeamNoFear

Day 354

TODAY'S WORD! Let not your heart be troubled; for greater is the gift we in Christ have been given. Sing songs of praise and rejoice, for hardships are only for a season. Let your light shine so that those in darkness may find their way to salvation. Lift your hands in worship, grateful for the blessings you have received in this life, and the one after. Awesome and mighty is the Lord our God whose Kingdom shall reign forever. #TeamNoFear

Day 355
TODAY'S WORD! Live your life with no regrets and continue to press forward in all you do. Lend a helping hand whenever possible and share a kind Word to build up your fellow man. In all things, give God thanks and rejoice, for he has given us joy. **#TeamNoFear**

Day 356
TODAY'S WORD! God has a plan for your life, and all things will work in your favor. Stay the course and maintain your faith, so that you may receive your reward. Look to the Lord our God for joy, so that your strength may be renewed. Continue to press forward for the victory is already ours, awesome and mighty is the Lord our God. **#TeamNoFear**

Day 357
TODAY'S WORD! Continue to press forward, knowing that the Lord our God has already made it well for us. Stay encouraged, and may your heart be filled with the joy of the Lord, for it is our strength. Remain focused on the task at hand, for you must get

239

your work done. Give thanks in all things and remain humble, for the Lord will reward you in due time. **#TeamNoFear**

Day 358
TODAY'S WORD! Submit to the Will of God, so that you may find yourself and move towards your destiny. Humble yourself under his mighty hand, so that you may be lifted in due time. Remain quiet so that you may receive your instructions to obtain the victory. Lift your hands in worship, so that the Lord our God is worshipped over all the earth. May you continue to press forward to obtain all that God has for you in this life. **#TeamNoFear**

Day 359
TODAY'S WORD! Let not the things of this world trouble you, for we are just passing through. Let not the words of your enemies find room in your heart, for they will only grow and cause you to fall. Find joy in your journey for the time continues to tick away with the passing of each day. May the Lord of our salvation continue to move us forward towards our

destiny and purpose. **#TeamNoFear**

Day 360

TODAY'S WORD! Fear not for the Lord our God is mighty in battle, and no enemy has a longer reach than he. All power and authority have been given to the Lord, our God, who holds healing in his hands. Sing awesome is the Lord our God, whose Kingdom is everlasting and mercy for all generations. Rejoice today, for salvation, is available to all who are willing to repent and receive it today. **#TeamNoFear**

Day 361

TODAY'S WORD! No man or woman can add one day to their life, nor can they extend time. Time is not a factor to the Lord our God, for he is everything, and his Will is perfect for us. Therefore, submit the life you have been given to him and commit the little time you have to him, so that your life may be complete. Awesome and mighty is the Lord our God whose Kingdom will reign forever. **#TeamNoFear**

Day 362

TODAY'S WORD! Today is a brand-new day! A chance to start again. An opportunity to make better decisions. Sit still and be quiet, to hear the voice of the Lord, so that you may receive your instructions to victory. Move forward in faith, knowing that victory is already yours at every turn. Lift your hands and give praise to the one and only God, the Lord of Host, our Savior, and the giver of life. **#TeamNoFear**

Day 363

TODAY'S WORD! Stay the course, keeping your faith intact, so that you may continue to move forward. Lean not to your understanding, but acknowledge the Lord in all your ways, and he will direct your path. Let not trouble cause you to stumble, nor lose your focus, for the work that has to be done is important. May these words find ground in your heart and bring forth one hundredfold. **#TeamNoFear**

Day 364

TODAY'S WORD! Let the words you speak build

up and not tear down. Let your conversations be spoken with love and your intents clear. Let your hands be found doing the work of the Lord, and your mind focus on the task at hand. Let your feet forever be firmly set on solid ground and may the Lord of our salvation continue to move us forward. #TeamNoFear

Day 365

TODAY'S WORD! There is no situation too difficult for our Lord to work out. The issue is with our lack of patience and our choosing not to sit still. We must learn to wait on God and move in his timing and within his plans. If we completely submit and commit to his Will, we are heading in the right direction to achieve maximum greatness. #TeamNoFear

If this book has indeed been a blessing to you, I ask that once you are done reading it, pass it on to someone who can benefit from these words of encouragement. *Bro. Ernest L Sledge.*

Reflections/Notes:

Reflections/Notes:

245

Reflections/Notes:

Reflections/Notes: